Loretta

"*The thrilling story of a dear and valued friend. I knew her personally for great portions of her life . . . This is a book that should be placed in every available hand.*"

Dr. C. M. Ward
Former voice of *Revivaltime*

"**One Witness,** *the story of Aggie Hurst, is a book that you will read with interest . . . She lived life to the fullest. All of us who knew her are blessed. This book will bless you.*"

Dr. G. Raymond Carlson,
General Superintendent
Assemblies of God

"*The story of Aggie Hurst is a gripping story you will not forget. Spanning three countries and as many cultures,* **One Witness** *speaks a message of providence, grace, love, forgiveness, and courage — and always in the superlative!*"

Philip Crouch, Vice President
Trinity Broadcasting Network

One Witness is the dramatic, delightful first-person account of Aggie Hurst. Born to Swedish missionaries in Africa, baby Aggie was given to an American missionary couple by her embittered father after the death of her mother. Eventually, the couple brought her to the States. Aggie struggled spiritually to make sense of her life; did God really know what He was doing when He brought her into the world? The ways in which God put together the puzzle pieces of her life make **One Witness** a fascinating, faith-building book. Aggie Hurst's triumphant story will show you how our Father truly does have a perfect plan for each life.

ONE WITNESS

AGGIE HURST
with DOUG BRENDEL

Published by 854
√ chosen books

FLEMING H. REVELL COMPANY
OLD TAPPAN, NEW JERSEY

Scripture quotations are from the King James Version of the Bible.

Library of Congress Cataloging-in-Publication Data

Hurst, Aggie.
  One witness.

    "A Chosen book"—T.p. verso.
    1. Hurst, Aggie.   2. Assemblies of God. General
Council—Biography.   3. Pentecostals—Biography.
I. Brendel, Doug.   II. Title.
BX6198.A78H873 1986   289.9 [B]   86–17876
ISBN 0-8007-9088-X

A Chosen Book
Copyright © 1986 by D. V. Hurst
Chosen Books are published by
Fleming H. Revell Company
Old Tappan, New Jersey
Printed in the United States of America

To
Arthur and Anna Berg
who chose me
and loved me
as their own

Contents

Contents

Foreword

Rarely does God create the kind of person Aggie Hurst was. He must get into a certain mood to mix this sort of concoction, the wit and the strength and the wisdom and the energy.

But the outcome is always a very special one. Friends of Aggie Hurst have never been ambivalent. Just say her name and things start to happen. Everything about Aggie has always been in high relief, in sharp contrast. No middle ground! No foot-dragging!

So often we let life drag us down. God never intended this—and Aggie energetically maintained otherwise. She was all the brightness and explosiveness that Christians should be, but seldom are. What a lively example of a lively faith!

I shall always be grateful for the wonderful interval of my own family's life that was shared with Aggie and hers.

They were enriching times, and not in any small way because of Aggie's presence and participation. Her wonderful, surprising, entertaining quality kept life interesting, which made learning even the hardest lessons an enjoyable experience.

Her story—and her very life—have touched countless ones around the world. I trust that now, through this book, her story will continue its marvelous work.

Dr. C. M. Ward
Scotts Valley, California

ONE WITNESS

1

The Death Child

You cannot conceive the many without the one.

—Plato

(How I happened to be born in Africa ... I didn't learn this story, of course, until many years after the events took place.)

David Flood looked up sharply at the tone in his friend Joel Erickson's voice.

"This is ridiculous," said Joel. His face was drawn tight with anger.

"What's ridiculous, Joel?" David asked.

"Everything! Coming to this God-forsaken continent. Traipsing through the jungles. Living like animals. Nearly killing our wives. And you've got little David who'll probably die of malaria."

David looked away from his friend and kicked at the African earth beneath his feet. He had been afraid of this moment. He had sensed Joel's emotional temperature rising almost from their first day in the Belgian Congo.

Reluctantly, David asked the question that had bothered him and his tiny wife Svea for months.

"What are you going to do?"

"You and Svea can stay if you want but Bertha and I are going back to the base." Joel spoke more softly. "The other missionaries are there, David. They're *veterans*. They know Africa. They're *accomplishing* something."

The words stung. David Flood did not reply, so his friend Joel continued building his case. "What have we to show for months of work? Malaria, malnutrition, two village chiefs furious with us—"

"There's the native boy," David answered quietly.

"Yes, the boy! Our one convert! For all these months, we have one conversion to report—a child, who probably doesn't understand a thing we say. I'm sorry, David. We have to go."

And he turned to find his wife and leave.

David Flood also turned, to look around at the mud hut home the four missionaries had built. He knew his friend was right. They had wandered into this wilderness, four innocents and a two-year-old boy. It had seemed such a fine thing to do. They rode on the wave of spiritual passion and missionary zeal—emotions that came naturally to them as members of the Philadelphia Church in Stockholm, Sweden. That venerable Pentecostal body had a renowned tradition of sending its young into the heathen world and winning lost souls to Jesus Christ.

As David stood surveying the ruins of his dream, he

14

could see the scenes of a few months before. There was that wonderful, almost mysterious missionary service at the Philadelphia Church, where he and Svea along with Joel and Bertha Erickson had simultaneously felt the call of God upon their lives directing them to head toward Africa. There was that thrilling day in 1921 when they had packed their belongings and set sail with little David for the Dark Continent.

There was the breathless arrival in Africa and the whirlwind of exotic scenes flashing and spinning around them as they made their way toward the interior of the Belgian Congo.

But there, the scenes in David Flood's mind began to be painful. He could recall how the gleam of an imagined destiny had begun to dim. Africa in 1921 was still a vicious continent. The Congo was aswarm with insects and animals never imagined in the most awful Scandinavian nightmare.

The natives clung tenaciously to their world view—they knew better than to anger their pagan gods by admitting these white monsters to corrupt their traditional values. David could still see the frowning face of the chief in the first village they reached.

"You cannot stay here."

"We will not harm you," David had tried to explain in his faltering Swahili. "We are here to help you."

"You do not help. You bring evil. Our gods grow angry. You cannot stay here."

And when David and Joel had hesitated, the chief had added ominously, "We will kill you. Go, *now*."

David could recall the aching of his muscles as the white people pressed through the jungles, hacking their way through thick trackless underbrush. He winced as he remembered the first sensations of malaria—the awful chills, followed suddenly by an internal firestorm. First one of them, then another, then the third—eventually all four adults and even David, Jr., had suffered the disease's terrifying symptoms. On the rare days when all five were healthy, they were able to drag themselves a little further into the mountain of the Congo.

As they approached the next village—N'dolera, on the side of a mountain—Bertha Erickson had begun to sob. David knew how she felt. They were all so tired from carrying their own supplies, so hungry, so terribly alone. Here, at N'dolera, they prayed that they could finally find rest, and the effective soul-winning ministry that they had traveled so far to achieve.

But the chief in N'dolera was more hostile than the last chief had been. Instead of using cold, measured words, this chief shouted and flailed his oily arms, his eyes blazing. David, Jr., had begun to cry, clutching at his mother's dress. The missionaries grasped their belongings and pushed once again into the outlying mountain jungle.

At that point Joel reached the end of his endurance, his eyes swimming with tears. "We cannot do this!" he said as they stumbled through the thick tropical bush. Bertha, too, was weeping.

"But we can't stay in N'dolera, either!" David Flood called, pushing on. Once again, he noticed it was only his little wife Svea who never complained.

Svea Flood—tiny, only four feet eight inches tall, but rugged—glanced at Bertha as if yearning to comfort her. But the two men were talking again, their faces shiny with perspiration, their almost white Scandinavian hair matted and filthy.

"Let's set up camp here," Joel said.

"Here?" David answered. "We'll be eaten alive by bugs and animals! And if not that, then the natives will discover us, and that will be the end."

"It's the end anyway!"

"It's the test," David maintained resolutely.

"It's a *mistake!*" Joel cried.

David looked down at Svea, then at Bertha. In Svea's eyes, David thought he could see resolve, determination to make good on the call that she and the rest believed so sincerely had come from God. But in Bertha's face was fear—and utter, bottomless exhaustion.

They needed time. Time to regroup. Time to let emotions settle. David looked at the terrain all around. They were headed down the mountain, back into the jungle valley beneath N'dolera. But if they climbed uphill instead they would have a clear view of the valley, and of any N'doleran villagers who might get the notion to ambush them. And the foliage, so thick and oppressive in the valley, looked thinner on the mountaintop.

Joel's blue eyes flashed as David suggested it.

"You said yourself we'll never make another village," David argued. "Not in our condition. We've got to stop—and we can't stop here. Let's climb the mountain. At least for tonight. And maybe we can establish some trade with N'dolera—food and supplies."

"Oh, David," Joel sighed, but he turned toward the mountain.

On they went, always upward, huffing and wheezing, malaria-ravaged missionaries struggling to carry their few supplies to the summit. They had pitched their tents that afternoon, then realized they were too weary to set out again in search of yet another village. So they decided to clear the brush and erect mud huts, doing their best with the hostile villagers of N'dolera. On faith, they actually erected a third mud hut, to serve as a church building and, when it was finished, whispered prayers that the humble structure would be filled to capacity with lively Africans.

During the next agonizing weeks, which stretched into agonizing months, the Floods and the Ericksons tried innumerable tactics to penetrate N'dolera. But the village chief had not relented. Instead, he tightened his grip on his people. The villagers were prohibited from even visiting the mountaintop. Only one little boy was allowed to go up—never more than twice a week—to sell chickens and eggs for whatever he could get. David smiled at his scrappy little wife's resolve to win that lone African boy to the Lord.

"If he's the only African God has given us, then we'll win him!" she announced to the rest of the missionary party.

"Oh, come now, Svea," Bertha said quietly. "He's just a boy. He has trouble following your Swahili."

"We're here to win *Africa!*" Joel said to Svea. Then he nodded toward N'dolera. "And we can't even win a single village."

"But Africa *one at a time*," Svea replied without missing a beat. "This child has a soul, and God loves him just as much as he loves any one of the millions on this continent."

Svea plunged into the task wholeheartedly. Each time the boy visited camp, she showered him with love. And sure enough, the day came when David saw her kneel beside the little black boy and lead him in a prayer of repentance. The boy accepted Jesus Christ as his personal Savior. He had to keep his decision secret in the village, but on the mountaintop, he shone with delight.

Svea wept with joy, but to the Ericksons the mission seemed like a failure. Day after day, the darkness seemed to grow, until there was no light in their eyes at all and Joel announced that they were leaving.

So now the two men stiffly embraced one another, and the women clung to each other for a final, tearful moment. The Ericksons set off down the mountain toward the well-established missionary outpost of Uvira.

As they watched, Svea Flood slipped her arm around her husband's waist.

But David Flood felt nauseous in spite of her comfort.

They might have left soon themselves, but for a complication. With a face full of swirling emotions, Svea advised her husband that they would soon have another child.

David realized what this meant. Svea was rugged, yes, but her first pregnancy—even in Sweden—had been harrowing. Travel through the jungles of the Belgian Congo could kill her now.

They had to wait. The baby would be born on the mountain.

The little native boy broke the news to the village. He was panting from making the trip down the mountainside in half the usual time. His eyes were wide and round.

"The white woman!" he cried. "She is going to have a baby!"

The entire village reacted with glee. None of them had ever seen a newborn white baby. In spite of the danger these foreigners were supposed to present, every person in the village was gripped with curiosity.

The chief magnanimously arranged for a woman in the village to travel up the mountain and act as midwife at the appointed time, partially to care for the mother and baby, but also to make sure the proper tribal customs were observed.

By the time the baby was due, Svea Flood was weak with malaria. The African midwife arrived on schedule from the village, but she found Svea groaning with fever. On Friday, the thirteenth of April, a baby girl was born. David wept for the little creature with almost no chance to live. Svea was too weak to weep anymore.

The midwife calmly cut the infant's umbilical cord, then carried it out of the hut. David watched as the woman knelt and began digging a hole in the earth with her hand. When it was deep enough, she gently placed the umbilical cord in the hole and covered it back up with African soil.

"Now," she said softly, "she will always be one of us."

David Flood stood tensely over his wife as she slipped in and out of consciousness. He touched her flaming forehead again and again, each time praying that the heat would have subsided, but the fever refused to break.

Finally Svea opened her eyes. "David," she gasped.

"Svea, my love, you've given us a girl."

"A girl!" Svea smiled weakly. "Call her Aina," she whispered. It was one of the classical Swedish names, pronounced "ah-ee-nah" with the beautiful lilt of the Swedish language. "Aina Cecelia," she added. Cecelia was the name of her younger sister back in Sweden.

David squeezed his wife's limp hand and agreed. The baby would be Aina Cecelia. The midwife would not look squarely at him as if she knew the end was at hand. Even in the steamy heat of the Congo, David felt his hands go cold.

Svea suffered for a week, then another week, and into a third. Two-year-old David, Jr., exulted over the birth of a baby sister, oblivious of his mother's condition. Meanwhile, tiny Svea Flood fought valiantly against the malaria. But finally, when little Aina was seventeen days old, death consumed Svea Flood.

It was impossible to transport Svea's remains to Sweden for burial. She would have to be buried in Africa.

Stunned, silent, his face streaked with the tears of hopelessness, David dug a crude grave. "What a waste of life," he groaned as he shoveled yet another mound of dirt. She had been one of the finest sopranos in the Philadelphia Church. She had the enviable quality of making people happy wherever she went, simply because her personal presence was so bright.

And now—gone.

David slid the homemade box into the earth, and wrapped himself in his own arms as he wept aloud. When he was able, he began the somber process of shoveling dirt back over the box, and as he stood over the finished task, he took stock of his life. He was twenty-seven years old. His beautiful wife had been taken from him. He could hardly care for his two-year-old son. And now a tiny, sickly baby girl had come along.

For the first time since coming to Africa a terrifying, vivid doubting crowded into his mind. He looked at little David standing near Svea's grave, and the doubt turned to anger. It welled up quickly, and grew at a furious pace. As he packed up his few belongings, he was engulfed by a resolute bitterness.

He had been faithful. He had willingly brought himself and his family into this backward world, ready to build the Kingdom by the sweat of his brow.

And for what? Death and desertion and desperation—and the salvation of only one little African boy.

David Flood marched into the village of N'dolera—they

would certainly not kill him now, and if they did, he didn't care. There he hired young African men as carriers. He was not about to drag himself single-handedly through that jungle again. Africans had created this nightmare; they could get him out of it.

One of the young men put baby Aina in a woven hammock he had made for the journey. Others carried David's belongings. The procession set out for Uvira, the mission station where the Ericksons had gone nearly a year earlier, with David alternately leading and carrying his son.

As for the hapless infant Aina, they stopped at each village and called for a "mama" to volunteer as a nurse. There was never a shortage of milk; the African mothers were fascinated by the little white baby, and it was the chance of a lifetime to nurse her.

The baby, thin and sickly as she was, refused to die, even after exposure to so much raw jungle. At three weeks of age, Aina had developed an uncommon will to live.

As Uvira came into view, David sent messengers ahead and soon the Ericksons, now looking fit and content, embraced their pitiful, shallow-cheeked friend. For a few days, they tried to make Uvira a bit like home for him and the children. But then, when they felt he could handle the subject, the Ericksons confronted David.

"You know you cannot go back," Joel Erickson began.

"Back to N'dolera?" David asked, incredulous. "Of course not."

"Back to Sweden," Joel corrected him.

David snapped to look at them both.

"Why not?"

"This post is the most developed place for hundreds of

miles," Joel replied. "To get from Uvira to the nearest port is a nightmare of a trip."

"I'll survive," David insisted.

"But Aina won't," Bertha broke in.

David did not look up. He did not answer.

"David, she is fighting for her life," Bertha continued. "The missionaries here are doing everything they can for her, but to take her back into that jungle—"

She turned her face away. "You may as well kill her outright."

There was a long silence. David could hear the steady breathing of his friend Joel, and he couldn't help but realize how healthy he sounded now, compared to that last long trip up the mountainside at N'dolera.

"Little David might make it," Joel finally said. "*Might*. But you can't take Aina. There aren't any wet nurses and—"

"All right! You've made your point. But I can't be a prisoner here at Uvira. I've got to start my life over again in Sweden. And not in ministry, either. Not after Svea."

Bertha shuddered. "Oh, David. Don't talk like this."

"It's more than that," David finally said. "I have to return to Sweden because I am losing my eyesight."

The Ericksons looked at each other sharply.

"It's in our family. I am going to need surgery to prevent cataracts from blinding me completely."

"David, I'm so sorry," Bertha whispered.

"There is another option," Joel said evenly. "We could keep Aina here, with us. We've discussed it."

David looked up at him and realized that this whole presentation had been carefully planned.

"We're going back on furlough next year," Bertha said.

"Aina would be strong enough to travel by then. We'll bring her back to you."

David knew they were offering a kindness, but he also knew they desperately wanted a child.

A week later, as the African carriers gathered once again, David Flood handed over his month-old daughter to Bertha Erickson. Little David had outgrown his shoes so they left them behind for Aina. She could wear them in a short time—if she lived. He put the infant into the arms of the missionary woman, took his son by the hand, turned sharply, and began walking fast.

He never looked back.

David Flood spent the voyage leaning disconsolately over the railing, staring into the water, aching over the loss of his sweet Svea, and brooding over God's unfairness.

David, Jr., played with abandon. But occasionally he stopped suddenly, as if for no reason, and looked around. Perhaps he was wondering where the baby was—and when he would hear her cry again.

He would wait more than forty years to hear her cry again.

2

Rescue and Ruin

The very ruins have been destroyed.

—Lucan

(*I am left in Africa while my father and brother return to Sweden . . . and move toward trouble.*)

The baby was a joy.

Uvira was one of those busy missionary outposts in the Congo, staffed mostly by Swedes, and located on Lake Tanganyika, which provided water transportation to a huge region. It was also a spectacular setting. From the palm-lined trail leading to the Uvira station, sunsets were glorious.

The Ericksons now operated the Uvira station, along with other missionaries. Some of the natives in the nearby village were Christian and cooperative. Of course there were pockets of hostility among the unconvinced Africans—the chief of the village was angry over the intrusion, but then he always had been. The missionaries had been threatened by him in times past, but nobody really took it seriously since Swedes had been working there for years and nothing bad had happened.

And now little Aina made Uvira all the more pleasant a place to live and work. Anyone passing through was delighted with the unexpected sight of a white-skinned baby girl.

The baby prospered. Everyone in the village doted over her, so she was never without attention and care. She was nine months old now and seemed to be on her way to a happy, healthy reunion with her father in Sweden.

But a gruesome turn of events cut short the plan. One day, while Bertha and Joel were finishing dinner, Bertha's eyes glassed over, and she began to cough violently.

"Bertha!" Joel cried. "What is it?"

She clutched her stomach and cried out, but she could not form words.

"God in heaven!" Joel screamed, leading his wife to the bed. "What is happening?"

Other missionaries came running, but there was no helping her. In moments, she was dead.

What had happened? Joel sat next to his wife's still body, stunned, refusing to accept her death. Finally he had no choice but to join the others in the sad task of preparing for a burial. Two old friends who were American missionaries, Arthur and Anna Berg, had stopped at Uvira several days earlier, and now Arthur—an expert carpenter—joined Joel in the work of building a simple coffin and digging a humble grave.

It was to have been a time of rest for the Bergs. Bespectacled Arthur, all of five feet tall, was an accomplished singer as well as a carpenter, and his wife Anna was stout-spirited and serious-minded. Joel and his Bertha had worked once, briefly, with these Americans who were stationed 'way north of Uvira, at Massisi. This childless family had been on their way to a mission station in the south when they stopped for rest at Uvira—and came upon tragedy.

The missionaries and many of the natives wept as Bertha's body was laid in the African earth, encased in its crude coffin. One person did not join in the mourning . . . the local chief. He stood apart from the rest, staring, arms folded across his chest.

As the memorial service drew to a close, the little band of missionaries returned to the Ericksons' quarters where Aina was asleep in her crib; and it was then that Joel Erickson did a most extraordinary thing. He scooped Aina into his arms, and headed toward the Bergs.

"God sent you here for this," he said directly, swallowing his tears.

They looked at him steadily. Little Aina lay in Joel's arms, sleeping.

"Anna," Joel said firmly to the American woman, "you have no children, but now you have a very special gift from God. Aina."

Anna and Arthur Berg looked at each other for a brief moment, but they had no need of conversation. Joel held the baby out and without a word Anna took the child in her arms, then cuddled her close.

Three days later death again screamed through the camp.

"Help me!" Joel Erickson shrieked from his room shortly after supper. Anna Berg was among the first to reach him; she found him clutching at his stomach. Anna ran to get her husband. Along with others from the base they alternated moistening Joel's face with a wet cloth.

Arthur Berg prayed in anguish as he watched his friend's torment.

What was happening? Why was this mysterious deadly force suddenly attacking them? He knew of no African illness that would create these symptoms. They had not eaten anything out of the ordinary. There had been no changes in the routine, nor the weather, nor—

Suddenly, Arthur remembered the scene at Bertha's burial, when the local chief had stood away from the mourners, his very posture bespeaking hostility.

Poison?

Joel Erickson did not last long.

Once again Arthur Berg found himself assembling a stark box for another corpse, this time the body of the man who had helped him, only hours before, build another box like it.

Even as the little band of missionaries conducted their funeral service for Joel Erickson, still another missionary felt the first pangs. Her stomach cramped and cramped again, bending her face down to her knees. She screamed, but she could not stop the onrush of death.

As Arthur and Anna Berg quickly left Uvira with little Aina, they left behind three fresh graves and a question they never did resolve: what was it that killed their companions? But it gave Anna all the more incentive to consider Aina as a very special charge.

Yes, Anna Berg would take care of Aina. What an unexpected blessing! She would take *wonderful* care of Aina!

And her first act of motherhood would be to change that odd Swedish name—Aina would become Agnes, after Arthur's oldest sister. And the child's friends would call her Aggie.

When the Bergs returned to their faraway northern village, Massisi, it was all the more curious to see a white child. Africans came from miles around to see her blue eyes, stroke her pale skin, touch her blond hair. They laughed and cooed at her, talking baby-talk in Swahili.

When Aggie began to talk, her new parents thought it wise to let her speak only the languages of the village, so the first words she learned were Swahili. At seventeen months she was speaking three dialects.

The noxious bacteria of Africa began to pursue Aggie, and she struggled again and again with illnesses. Rickets, the bone-bending disease so long associated with Africa, was a particular problem. Aggie's right ankle tended to turn in as the rickets attacked her—and yet, again and again, the prayers of her new parents turned back the evil tide of sickness.

She was slow to walk, perhaps because of the rickets. But a thoughtful old African man happened up the trail one day and whimsically offered her a simple handmade cane. Immediately she stood up, leaning on the cane like a senior citizen. Soon she was walking normally.

So, for the most part, Aggie knew nothing but fun and friends—countless little African friends. Together they ate roasted crickets and played games with gourds and ran naked in the sun. She loved those funny shoes that her parents said came from a place called Sweden, and she played in them often, even before she grew into them. But barefoot was always better.

One day a friend of Anna's from Chicago sent Aggie an

actual doll—a thrilling day not only for Aggie but for the entire African community, never having seen a doll before!

So, for all Aggie knew, she was in Paradise. She had no concept of the sorrow that had gone on before her.

And she had no concept of the problems to come.

Meanwhile, Aggie's natural father had arrived safely in Sweden. Now a bitter, angry man, he began to look for someone who would help carry his hurt. His dear Svea had two sisters—an older one, Signe, who had also given herself to missions and was already in Brazil; and a younger unmarried sister, Cecelia, back in Stockholm.

He could marry her, if she would have him, and begin life again.

Cecelia was more than happy to respond to overtures from David Flood. Since he had returned from Africa, he had opened an import business and although he was not doing well, she remembered him from the days when he was Svea's husband, and he seemed then to be a fine young man. She did not know that David Flood was no longer anything like she remembered.

They were married and the grief began almost immediately. David discovered that he did not know Cecelia at all. Far from being the cheerful, positive character Svea had been, Cecelia was a negative, ingrown person, consumed with her problems. David, no longer the willing enthusiast for God's worldwide work, was corroded by bitterness, determined never to return to the ministry, convinced that he should spend his life making money and enjoying it—a formula that seldom produced money, and never enjoyment.

David learned to drink, and did a lot of it. His rantings made Cecelia ever more miserable. Two baby boys were born of the Floods and they, along with the older boy

David, Jr., lived in turmoil. Cecelia vented her anger on David, Jr., who didn't take long to become a morose little child. He took to leaving the house in the morning, seldom returning before dark. In the summertime, she sent him out to the country, to David's younger twin brother and sister, Uncle Reuben and Aunt Anna, who had never married and lived on the lake in Karlsborg above their antique shop. Reuben's peculiar vice was that he played slot machines as often as he could. Other than this odd trait, there was nothing but stability at Reuben and Anna's. David, Jr., spent summers with them and one day he came to the antique shop to stay. Reuben and Anna led the kind of pacific life he longed for. He did not want to become what his father had become—a widower first, and then an alcoholic railer, making his second wife wish she were a widow.

And David, Senior? As he stared into glass after glass of liquor, David Flood was a haunted man. God had duped him into going to Africa, then had taken his wife, and forced him to leave a daughter behind. Now he had made the mistake of marrying this woman, and the house was full of babies once again. His own eldest son was a virtual outcast. David Flood's world was a shambles. One had only to mention the name of God and his anger exploded into curses.

And then the letter came.

It was from the Belgian Congo, and David Flood knew, even as he opened it, what it would say.

31

3

Paying Mommie Back

Home is the place where, when you have to go there,
They have to take you in.

—Robert Frost

(*I become something of a curiosity, a child Tarzan*
straight out of the trees of Africa.)

It came time for Arthur and Anna Berg to leave Africa,
but little Aggie was a problem. They could not take a child
who was not legally their own out of the country. And getting conditional custody proved to be a nightmare of red
tape. The Congo could issue no papers since it was only a
colony of Belgium. The Belgian government had no interest in the little girl; she, after all, was a Swedish child. In
Sweden, the government thought it was an open-and-
closed case; since she had no passport or birth certificate,

33

the biological father must have complete say in the matter. Arthur Berg appealed to his own government; they could do nothing, for Berg's American citizenship really had nothing to do with the question of Aggie's. She was a girl without a country.

It was clear to Anna Berg that David Flood was unfit to rear the girl. He had made no known attempt in more than two years to communicate with her first foster parents, the Ericksons, or with her accidental foster parents, the Bergs. Occasionally Swedish missionaries brought news of the Stockholm Philadelphia Church—but never news of David Flood. He had long since fallen by the wayside. He no longer darkened Philadelphia's doors.

The whole affair disgusted Anna Berg—and at the same time wedded her to little Aggie more thoroughly. She felt she should be this child's mother for life, and it frightened her when she imagined David Flood suddenly coming to his senses and moving in to reclaim his long-lost daughter.

So she resisted the notion of writing David Flood for permission to take Aggie to America with them. What if he said no? What if he used the opportunity to insist that they ship her back to him, even after two years of neglect?

Without telephones, without telegraph, the Bergs slaved away at the project through the sluggish international mails of the 1920s, writing long, hopeful letters, and then waiting endlessly for replies from government underlings thousands of miles away. The process was nerve-wracking, and each time a foreign letter arrived in the mail, their hearts stalled until the contents were digested. But the contents never brought an end to the drama: no one could give them permission to take Aggie with them to America.

Finally, as her third birthday approached, the Bergs

faced the inevitable unpleasant task. They would have to try the least preferred option: they would have to write David Flood.

David Flood looked at the world around him and snorted derisively. It was no place for a little girl. It was hardly a place for him!

He tore a stained piece of paper off of a dog-eared writing tablet and scratched out a reply to the Bergs' letter: "You have my permission to take Aina to America."

Then he signed the letter, sealed it in an envelope, and blinked back tears as he dropped the letter in the mailbox.

Three-year-old Aggie celebrated with her African playmates as they saw her off for the coast. She would be taking a long trip on a big boat. What adventure!

It was several days' journey to the port where the big boat would pick them up. The strong young African men carried all the belongings—with Aggie swinging along in a hammock—through the brush, each night setting up camp, covering her with mosquito netting, making sure she was comfortable. She was a Jungle Queen, living it up.

The ship was a wonderful playground. Even with no common language (Aggie still spoke only Swahili) Aggie captivated the crew and other passengers. There were innumerable playthings on such a vessel, and Aggie tinkered with them all. She became a crack three-year-old competitor in shuffleboard, a game she had never seen before. The other children on the voyage were a whole new frontier for her. And when the children had a party, Anna Berg made sure Aggie won the prize for best costume by sewing rows of crepe paper in ruffles on her dress.

35

Aggie squealed with glee at the Statue of Liberty in New York Harbor. The Bergs could not afford a hotel room so they stayed at a missionary rest home in the city. Anna, in the flush of excitement at being home, took her young darling to a department store and bought her the classic American plaything: a huge teddy bear. In the coming months, it would be her anchor in a swirling, frightening foreign world.

They traveled by train from New York to Minneapolis, Arthur Berg's home. The train ride for Aggie was a marvelous combination of sights and sounds. But it was in Minneapolis, as her mother carried her out the door of the train car, that the nightmare began.

A crowd of friends and relatives had gathered at the depot to welcome the threesome back home. They all knew that the Bergs were bringing a little one with them, and excitement ran high. A huge banner stretched across the entryway: "Welcome Arthur & Anna Berg & little Aggie." The crowd was boisterous, hollering and cheering madly. As the Bergs stepped off the train, the people pressed around them for a glimpse of the child. They reached out to touch her, to grab her, to talk to her, curious to see what the Bergs had brought back from the Dark Continent.

For the first time in her life Aggie was petrified. Now her adoptive parents' decision to speak only Swahili in their home gave them second thoughts. Aggie began screaming and crying out in Swahili, and the crowd was silenced. Her mother tried to shush her, which only made her cry more hysterically.

The Bergs decided to move in with Arthur's mother for a few weeks until their future was decided. Living in the house already were four other relatives—Arthur Berg's sister and her husband and their daughters of about Aggie's age, little Ruth and Irene. The whole ménage was run, orchestrated, by one person ... Grandmother Berg.

Into this household came the Swahili refugee, unable to communicate in English, unaware of any but African customs. From the very first the chemistry was wrong.

Grandmother Berg met her son and his unusual family at the door of her house on 16th Avenue. She reached out to the terrified Aggie, scooped her into her arms, and carried her off toward her rocking chair, jigging as she went. Aggie barely had time to cry before Grandmother Berg, a saintly, albeit imposing, woman was rocking her energetically and chattering. Aggie had never seen a rocking chair before, had never seen this woman before, and had never been confronted at such close quarters with another language. She promptly began wailing. Grandmother stopped rocking, her well-intentioned efforts thwarted, and set the child on the floor.

"Arthur," she said to her son, "come take this child."

Arthur picked Aggie up and comforted her while he explained the problem. Aggie continued to cry, cementing the family's notion that she was perhaps a strange child.

Aggie's beautiful life was over.

She learned English slowly, and learned the American way of life—an abrupt adjustment for a three-year-old African girl. She cried a lot. She felt ill. She wanted to go home. Home to the Congo.

Her new fears were fed by everyone right down to the baby-sitters who threatened that if she wasn't good her "mean dad from Sweden" would kidnap her. The threat would terrify Aggie into immediate submission.

Grandmother Berg, a devoted Christian (who never

37

missed a church service until she broke her hip at the age
of ninety-three), tried hard to warm up to Aggie, including
her in her two little cousins' tea parties and buying all
three of them popsicles. Bit by bit Ruth and Irene became
Aggie's friends. They learned to ride bikes together,
sneaked into parsonage weddings together. But Aggie always had the sense that she was not one of the group; she
was "the little girl Arthur and Anna found in Africa." She
was the odd one, not quite family and not quite visitor.

Anna Berg's mother, Grandma Hanson, was a great
bright spot for Aggie. Grandma Hanson loved her instantly. To her, Aggie was just a little girl, full of life and
love and wonderful potential.

When Aggie was almost four years old Arthur Berg
moved to Sisseton, South Dakota, to begin working with
Indians on a reservation. It was a storefront operation,
with the preacher's family living upstairs using curtains for
room dividers and apple boxes for furniture. They held
services every single night. Aggie passed out songbooks,
raked sawdust, dusted benches, and was remanded to a cot
in the dark furnace room for naps during Papa's sermons.
She actually spent the time peeking out through a crack in
the door. When her mother came to get her at the end of
the service, she pretended to be sleeping.

Later Arthur Berg started another church in Sioux Falls,
South Dakota. At missions conventions, Arthur and Anna
were invariably called upon to tell the amazing story of
Aggie's rescue from the wild jungles of the Congo. Aggie
heard her story again and again from the platform until
she herself was walking through the sad deaths and disap-
pointments.

Aggie discovered she could sing. Whenever Anna told the amazing story and Aggie followed by singing "Tell Mother I'll Be There," the missionary offerings were large, and the altars were filled with sincere teary-eyed listeners.

But even these highlight moments served to make Aggie an oddity. When in her travels she met her by-now-close-friends Ruth and Irene, she never failed to notice that her cousins were growing up "normally" while she remained a curiosity. Once, after a service at the Lake Geneva Camp in Alexandria, Minnesota, Aggie headed for the snack shack with Ruth and Irene for an ice cream cone. There she overheard a few adults from the evening's audience whispering excitedly: "Look! She eats ice cream just like us!" Aggie looked around to see whom they were talking about. Suddenly her face turned red; she realized they were discussing her.

The problem didn't go away, even long after she had become Americanized. Especially after her story was told in a public meeting, she often sensed the alienation. If she kicked a stone on the street, it was a surprise to people. If she laughed at a joke, it was an event. And each time she heard a comment or saw a strange look on someone's face, she instinctively responded by asking herself, "What's wrong with me? Aren't I like other kids?"

She sometimes heard similar types of comments in her own family. If she was naughty, someone was sure to tell her parents that she must have a bad streak in her blood. On their frequent visits to Minnesota, when Grandmother Berg had her alone, she often asked Aggie the question that came to disquiet her the most: "How are you ever going to pay back Arthur and Anna for what they've done for you?" Aggie could only bottle up her sadness awhile;

then she would run to her daddy and fling her arms around him and ask him, "How in the world am I ever going to pay you and Mommie back!"

Arthur chuckled every time. "Children don't pay their mommies and daddies back. They just love them. Where'd you ever get such a silly notion?"

"Oh, I don't know," she always responded. She could never reveal the uncomfortable truth.

Aggie's mother was too trusting to doubt or question reports of Aggie's behavior. Anna Berg was a proper Pentecostal girl from 'way back. Her father, the Rev. C. M. Hanson, had been filled with the Spirit in 1896, long before the experience was widespread. (He became the first superintendent of the North Central District of the Assemblies of God.) Anna's life was directed toward keeping everyone around her perfectly happy. With her every action, even as a young adult, she labored to please people.

Which played a role in Aggie's upbringing. If a mother in the church reported that Aggie had stuck out her tongue, Anna was not above leaving her place on the church organ bench, taking her daughter out of the service, spanking her, and seating her again in her place, all without explanation. When the church's only hairdresser made Aggie look like a cross between Shirley Temple and Aunt Jemima, Anna insisted that Aggie thank the woman and return to her next time as well. All her anger was bottled up inside, never expressed, not even when, as she grew older, Ruth and Irene's mother asked Aggie to wash the dishes at family get-togethers. Anna could not think of protesting on behalf of her daughter, so Aggie stood at the sink alone while Ruth and Irene played elsewhere.

Anna wanted her daughter to excel, to make everyone

proud of her. So Aggie sang solos and sang with the choir and played the violin. To fail to meet someone else's expectations was taboo.

Because Aggie was not especially healthy, her mother dictated an eight o'clock bedtime every evening. Even in summer, when the sun was still shining, Aggie was sent to her bed at eight. She could hear the other children playing outside, and her playful spirit made her ache to join them. But even though it hurt, deep inside she knew her mother, to whom she owed so much, was trying to take good care of her.

The swallowing of her anger over a period of years gave Aggie real problems with digestion. Her health became an obsession with her mother who had feared so for her life as an infant. "You don't look well," her mother would say. "Do you have a fever?" Or, "You need a sweater." Eventually Aggie learned that she could feign illness easily, and that it was the perfect out when it came time for some unpleasant task. So she spent much of her time lying down, sometimes uneasy because she knew she had fibbed and really felt fine.

In the process, Aggie made no close friends. She was growing up isolated from others her age by her constant activities and her long hours in the sickbed.

Rarely, however, does a child go long without friends. The inventive mind of little Aggie concocted friends of her own.

She made up a family of brothers to play with.

4

Brothers
Real and Otherwise

*Without friends no one would choose to live, though he
had all other goods.*

—Aristotle

(*At last I can begin telling my own story.*)

I knew from hearing my own story told so many times in
so many church services that I had a brother named
David. He lived somewhere in Sweden, if he was still alive.

But I had a second brother named David, who was imaginary. I created him during one of those long summer evenings, after my mother had put me to bed before the sun
went down. I lay in my bed, and my mind went to work.

First I put a face on my imaginary David. He was good-
looking, dark-haired. Then I dressed him. He was quite
tall, and athletic in build. I made him helpful and protec-

43

tive and loving. David and I did everything together and he always took care of his little sister Aggie. When in real life kids threatened me at school, I could always scare them off by telling them that my big brother David would come along at any moment and make hamburger out of them!

Since I spent plenty of time in that bed, my imaginary family inevitably began to grow. Sundays were the most fertile time for imagining because after Sunday dinner I had to take a nap (which, incidentally, none of my friends endured).

So, mostly on Sundays, I made wonderful additions to my imaginary family. David was followed by Joseph, who was even better-looking. Joseph had all the girl friends. They were always calling him on the phone.

Then came my third imaginary brother Gene, who wasn't really living for the Lord. He was big and husky. At school I once chose him as the subject of a composition. I wrote that our home was like Grand Central Station, with laughter and activity going on all the time, and a huge table in the dining room, which could have any number of hilarious characters around it each evening at mealtime. Once, I wrote, Gene came home thirty minutes late, a real taboo in my fabricated house. Accordingly, I wrote, my mother denied him supper. But Gene had an excuse. He had come home on a newly purchased motorcycle.

"I didn't know how to turn the dumb thing off," Gene protested, "so I drove it around till I ran out of gas!"

In the story, my father exploded into laughter and declared, "I've never heard a better excuse! Mother, you'd better feed the boy."

Stephen was the last of my imaginary family of four boys and one girl (me), and he was the mama's boy, the one who always tattled on the rest of us. He whined a lot. But Stephen had one redeeming value: he would play dolls with me, and none of the other boys would.

I talked to my brothers aloud, and my mother often stood at the foot of the stairs and called up to ask me whom I was talking to. I claimed I was talking to the dog.

In the real world, I went so far as to collect readily available photos of GIs from our church's GI camp and tell my friends that these guys were my brothers.

I had no idea that all four of my imaginary "brothers" were real, and that one day I would meet them face-to-face.

Ten thousand miles away, and of course unknown to me yet, more children were added to the real Flood family. David, Jr., was by now living off in Karlsborg with his father's twin brother and sister, Uncle Reuben and Aunt Anna. David, Jr., had been followed by a second baby brother, Joseph. A third son followed Joseph. His name was Don, and he somehow managed to grow up jolly and carefree. The kind who might drive a motorcycle till he ran out of gas.

Restless and irritable, drinking heavily now, my father David Flood moved his family to Gothenburg, two hundred miles from Stockholm, hoping to build more business. There, his wife became pregnant again, and grew weaker and weaker throughout the pregnancy. A very tiny baby girl, Ingrid, was born.

I never did learn why my natural father, David Flood, gave away this second of his two daughters. But I have often imagined what it was like for him. I could see him looking at tiny Ingrid through the hospital glass. A few yards away, his second wife, Cecelia, lay ill, nurses attending her. David's heart might have thumped heavily in his chest as the horrifying memories of Africa pressed in upon him again. A frail baby girl, a wife desperately sick, a hopelessness beyond description.

It looked like an obvious thing to do, to turn Ingrid over to a local couple, just until Cecelia was up and around and could care for the baby herself.

The Andreasens, solid Baptist people, were happy to take the baby in. Their own daughters were approaching their teens and this Ingrid would be a lovely addition to their home at just the right time.

Cecelia's recovery was slow. Before she could convalesce completely, David Flood folded his Gothenburg business and declared that the family would return to Stockholm. Months later, Cecelia finally felt strong enough to care for the baby but David always found an excuse not to retrieve the child.

Cecelia could not change his mind. She grieved for her lost daughter daily, and her health began to falter again. Mrs. Andreasen, fearful of losing her Ingrid, never told the child that she had a family full of brothers only two hundred miles away. But Mrs. Andreasen knew the story of the little child left in Africa, Aina Flood, and she fascinated Ingrid by telling her how she had a big sister who lived in America. Ingrid was fond of unrolling a large map of North America and driving a toy car over to see her big sister. She often told her friends about her big sister Aina in America. And every night Ingrid prayed for her big sister—and prayed that someday she would find her, "because sisters should always be together."

A fourth and final brother was born to Cecelia and David Flood. They called him Bengt. He grew up whiney and shy, a mama's boy.

The real-world replica of my imaginary family was now complete. Yet the real-world family was tragic and full of drama past even my imagining.

Cecelia Flood died of a broken heart, and her husband coped with his houseful of children by allowing a sympathetic woman to move in as his mistress. Martina would never marry David Flood; she would only love him genuinely and take care of his every need.

5

Sins

There is no witness so dreadful, no accuser so terrible as the conscience in the heart of every man.

—Polybius

Like Cecelia Flood, like Mrs. Andreasen, my adoptive parents in Minnesota were also struggling to keep from having their child snatched away. They could not adopt me officially because my natural father might—so said the law—still choose one day to take me back. And the immigration authorities had their rules. I was in the United States on a temporary visa. My father tried desperately with one goverment agency after another to find some way to keep me in the United States permanently. As it was I was required to leave United States territory and reenter under the approval of border guards. Every six months my father struggled with the bureaucrats to get extensions on my visa, postponing the trip. Finally, after the fifth extension, when I was six years old, the immigration official made it clear that there would be no more extensions.

We'd have to go to Canada and reenter if we could. The trip was nerve-wracking. As we prepared to drive to Canada (although my parents tried to be reassuring) I imagined that uniformed officials would seize me and lock me up forever. My stomach knotted up for days in advance of the trip, contributing to an ulcerated colon that would never completely disappear.

Finally, though, after eternal moments of tension, we were handed a new temporary "alien resident" visa and allowed to pass back into the U.S. And the horror was over ... until the next time.

I could see the tension and exasperation in my dear mother's face. I could see them slaving to keep me, and it anchored more certainly my determination never to cross them, never to question them, never to let my mother know if any portion of the life they were providing for me was making me unhappy. I must keep swallowing my hurt. These people were giving their lives for me.

In fact, in later years, I would learn why Arthur and Anna Berg never returned to the mission field: they could not be sure of keeping me if they ever left the country for an extended period of time. Missions had been their first love. They had dedicated themselves to missions before God, as a young couple. But for me, they gave it up. They cherished me that much. As a child, I never understood the depth of that love. They spent innumerable nights of vigil, through really dangerous fevers and infections. They gave themselves to me wholly and they never expressed a moment's regret. Their love ran deep and true and faithful. It was almost as if I had become the new work that God had given them. And they gave themselves to this new work with the same ceaseless devotion that had compelled them to Africa in the first place.

From what I later learned it appears that David Flood was alternately rational and irrational. One day he seemed to be content with his life and the next day he was aching with hurt and frustration. Martina cared for him consistently, despite his verbal abuse, but the steady care did not make him any steadier.

One day, while brooding over his sad past, he resolved to find that little girl he had left behind in the Congo so many years before. His mind was doubtless hazy with alcohol as he set up the old typewriter on the kitchen table. Then he began wringing out his best available facsimile of spiritual language that was designed to get him into the States.

"Praise the Lord, my brother Berg, in all things! My wife, Cecelia, and I desire to do the will of the Lord in coming to the U.S. and working with our brothers in the Lord in evangelistic endeavors. We entreat you to make yourself available to us as a sponsor: your signature below is all that we require. . . ."

The letter was received calmly in our house. My parents were very trusting people, particularly when it came to the things of the Lord, and David Flood's stated intention of doing evangelistic work in the United States was, as far as they were concerned, a more honorable one than they could ever think of questioning. My father even told me it was wonderful that I would finally get to meet my natural father. But I cried; I was afraid to meet this unknown figure from my past.

The shock waves did come, though, when my father lost the letter. It was sitting on his desk—he was sure of that—and suddenly it was gone. We scoured the house looking for it, but for all our panicky searching, none of us could turn it up.

That letter in fact never did reappear but a second letter arrived three days later. This one was from my Aunt Signe who was my natural mother's older sister. Aunt Signe, the missionary in Brazil, had heard from family of David Flood's proposal to come to the United States.

Aunt Signe sounded an alarm. David Flood, she warned, did not want to bring his wife to the United States for any sort of evangelistic work. In fact, Signe wrote, his wife Cecilia was dead. He was coming to take Aina—beware!

My mother trembled as she read the letter. She might have trusted David Flood and lost her precious daughter. My father wondered if he should even respond—he worried that any communication with a member of my biological family would weaken his case if we ever ended up in court. He waited weeks before writing her a brief thank-you note.

The David Flood letter never turned up. He never wrote again.

The special tensions of childhood were balanced by special blessings. My father had a radio program on a local station, so I got to sing on the radio every day. Cimba, my bulldog, was always right there with me. Cimba was a gift from a friend of the family who had come to the house one day and suggested that I reach into her coat pocket. I pulled out this marvelous little creature—a tiny puppy, its eyes not even yet open. I fed Cimba through the night with an eyedropper. As the dog grew, he became one of my closest friends, running alongside whenever I went biking, and guarding my bicycle when I reached my destination!

My father arranged for all the "great" preachers of the day to come to our church in Sioux Falls. I proudly gave up my bedroom to them—it seemed that others slept in it more than I did—and I curled up on a couple of blankets in the bathtub. I was delighted to do my duty. I was also absorbing great gobs of faith as these wonderful men and women of God brought their special brand of ministry into our home. In years to come, in times of stress, that deep faith would blossom.

My father continued wrangling with congressmen and judges to make my status permanent instead of temporary. The fight dragged on for years, until finally I had lived with them long enough—with no further contact from my father—that the government acknowledged what was already fact and cleared the way for the Bergs to adopt me legally.

There was no celebration that the event had finally occurred. Only a sense of immense relief, on the part of everyone.

A new excitement came into my life when John and Sam moved in. Their widowed mother needed a place to live, so the Bergs made part of their upstairs into an apartment. My parents were ceaseless boosters of the unwanted and unloved. Just as they scooped me up in Africa, so they continued helping the outcast throughout their lives, and taught me to do likewise.

For four years, John and Sam were my comrades. We explored realms of mischief previously unexplored.

Once a month my father offered Communion in his church. John and Sam and I were responsible for filling communion cups the night before and we decided we were entitled to drink a little of the grape juice. To make up for the losses we diluted the juice before pouring it into tiny individual cups.

One Saturday night, we got carried away with our sampling and when we diluted the skimpy remainder of the juice, it turned a pale pink. John and I ran home to lift some red and blue food coloring. We returned with the supplies, but none of us could figure out the right combination of colors.

The next morning, we sat shoulder-to-shoulder in the second row, watching diligently for the expression on my father's face when he removed the lid and looked at the cups. He did a classic double-take. The juice was blood-red, but he never said a word.

We enjoyed secret swims in the baptismal tank whenever a baptism was planned for the following day. When we once made the mistake of letting Cimba swim with us, our crime caught up with us as my father pulled the first participant out of the water. His white robe was covered with black dog hairs.

John and Sam would often rescue me from boredom when I was stationed in my bedroom while it was still light. They could climb out of their bedroom window and into mine by walking across the narrow roof. We whiled away many evenings eating fudge or popcorn sitting on the roof. Mother never caught me. She never opened the door to check on me; she was too trusting.

My two friends meshed nicely with my four imaginary brothers. They were amused by the whole idea, and they didn't mind it when I introduced them to my friends at school as my brothers. As long as I didn't tell my friends that their names were John and Sam, nobody was ever the wiser.

And one of the best parts was confusing our friends by telling them that my mother had never had a baby. John and Sam, who understood my situation, could back up my claim—and our schoolmates went crazy trying to figure it out.

Sam and John were my ticket to adventure, not to mention naughtiness—the two of which were synonymous for me. My bicycle-riding was restricted to the stretch between 13th Street and 4th Avenue. But with John and Sam, I sometimes went as far as 26th or 27th, an exhilarating distance, and always as fast as we could pedal.

One day John and Sam and I decided to experiment with the great taboos of our day—cosmetics and jewelry. (We avoided alcohol and tobacco, which were also taboos, because we believed they really were sinful.) My father had preached a sermon with lipstick as an illustration, waving an actual tube of the stuff before us during his sermon, and afterward accidentally leaving it in the pulpit. We retrieved it and took it up on the roof, where we either laid waste to my father's theology or forever condemned ourselves to hell.

The burden of secret naughtiness, of course, was a heavy one. When ladies at church patted me on the head and said how good I was, my conscience chided: "They don't know you on the inside!"

It was one of the multiple pressures of my status as combination preacher's kid, only child, and African refugee. If at the end of my father's sermon I went to the altar, someone always figured I had backslidden. If I didn't go to the altar, I should because I must need the Lord. If I cried at the altar, someone invariably wondered what Aggie had done this week. If I knelt with my head in my arms, I was really having a problem, and they wondered what it was. Sometimes church people stood around me at the end of every service waiting to offer counsel—only first they wanted to hear my confession. Perhaps I was overly suspicious, but I became quite skilled at ducking their questions with responses like, "I'll just have to keep praying about it" and "The Lord will just have to see me through." Afterwards, secretly, I would laugh. But it didn't feel good. And I wondered, in the depths of myself, what was wrong with me that made me do these things.

There was only one person I could ever ask.

6

A Top-Notch Boy

Women are wiser than men because they know less and understand more.

—James Stephens

There was only one surprise in my mother's protective care for me. Inexplicably, she allowed me to have a boyfriend.

His name was Ward Drake. We met in grade school, and by junior high we were constant companions. In high school he took to picking me up in the morning and walking me home at the end of the day. On many evenings he stayed for supper, and we often went to a ball game—if we didn't stay home and play table games until 9:30 when my mother sent me off to bed.

And it was during the many long, easy hours together that I had the freedom to expose the feelings that haunted

me: Why did my first mother die in Africa, Ward? Why
didn't my father come back for me? Ward, why hasn't my
older brother ever tried to contact me?

Ward could understand some of my turmoil. He had
a stepfather who had never agreed to adopt him legally so
all of his brothers were Swensons. Embarrassed Ward
changed his name to Swenson at school. Only I knew the
truth.

Ward responded to my questions by putting his arm
around me and smiling. "Well," he said, "all I can say is I'm
glad the Bergs brought you to America."

But his soothings never stilled my questions for long. I
wanted to know what was wrong with me, why I had
turned into an oddity.

The deepening relationship was snapped shortly after
my high school graduation when Ward's stepfather was
killed in an automobile accident in the nearby Black Hills.
His mother moved the family to California, and my open,
honest relationship came to an end. I wept bitterly for
days, writing agonizing letters to my lost friend and confidant. For a few months the exchange continued, until I
finagled a trip to California and went to visit Ward. He had
grown as sophisticated as the West Coast; I was still a
Midwest bobby-soxer. It was a pleasant vacation, but
Ward and I were no longer on the same wavelength.

Our communication grew sporadic after that, and when
he was drafted into the service a few months later, we lost
track of each other.

I missed him. But by then, it didn't matter quite as
much. My cousin Irene had picked out someone else for
me.

* * *

My old friends from early childhood, cousins Ruth and Irene, were both attending North Central Bible College over in Minneapolis and Irene had met Dewey Hurst, also a student there. Irene wrote me and admonished me not to cry over Ward Drake—Dewey, she figured, would be the perfect replacement.

I wasn't so sure. But a visit to Minneapolis would be fun nevertheless.

Ruth was not on campus when I arrived, but cousin Irene greeted me and immediately led me toward the Sunday afternoon chapel service. As we approached the door of the church she stopped and bent down to me.

"There he is," Irene whispered excitedly. There standing in the doorway was a skinny young man, passing out song books. I tried to keep from laughing and headed for two empty seats. "You gotta be kidding, Irene! He's just a kid!" Dewey Hurst looked to me as though he could not have weighed more than 125 pounds.

After chapel we paid the obligatory visit to the campus snack shack. Irene, still scheming, arranged for Dewey to visit our table and have Cokes with us. He arrived with a girl who I took to be his girlfriend. It was a ridiculous pairing; she was easily four years older than he was. She looked like his mother! Her hairdo and speech patterns disgusted me.

When we left, I gave Irene my assessment of the couple: "They're weird."

That was that. Dewey Hurst was obviously not for me. But I noticed that the name Dewey Hurst turned up on our church calendar the following month, traveling with a quartet from school. The day their gray car and trailer pulled up to our house, I was washing my father's car in scruffy jeans and a dirty sweatshirt, my hair wrapped in a bright red bandana.

"Hi, guys!" I called out, oblivious to my appearance and caring little about their reaction. "You're looking for my dad? His office is right in there, to the left."

And I kept on working.

When I was done, I went inside, bathed and dressed, set the table for my mother, and helped feed the pack of hungry boys.

Whenever I looked up from my food, it seemed, Dewey Hurst was looking at me.

After the evening's service (the quartet sang very well, indeed) the boys returned to our house and Dewey and I found ourselves alone in the living room.

"Would you do something for me?" he asked.

"Well," I responded, wondering where he was going, "if I can."

"Would you sign an application for North Central?"

I looked at his eyes, to see if he was joking. "You mean Bible college?" I started laughing. "Oh, lordy! They'd never let me come to Bible college!"

"I think they would," he replied softly, "and I think you'd enjoy it."

The boy was dead serious. I stopped laughing and looked at him for a moment.

"I'll give it some thought," I finally answered.

Later, after Dewey and his friends left, I did give his crazy idea some thought. There were certain strengths to the idea. Like most teenagers I thought it would be great fun to be away from home. And my folks—yes!—they would certainly like the idea.

When I asked Mother, her eyes filled with tears. "Oh,

honey," she exclaimed quietly, "this is just an answer to prayer."

Weeks passed. Since, in addition to pastoring the church in Sioux Falls, my father also served as Superintendent of the South Dakota Asssemblies of God, I always participated in the Assemblies' summer camp program. That summer, who should arrive at camp but Irene, and who should she bring *with* her but Dewey's girlfriend Phyllis.

As mischievous fate would have it, I was the camp's mail girl. Each day when the mail arrived I sorted it and distributed it. Today, there was a surprise in the mail—a letter with Dewey Hurst's name and return address scrawled in the upper left corner. The letter was addressed, of all things, to *me*.

Goodness! I said to myself. *What's he writing me for?*

I shoved the envelope deep into my pocket and continued my work. Soon, to my delight, Phyllis came to dig through the mail. As she searched, she squealed, "I wonder if there's a letter from my sweetie? I told him I'd be here today."

Wouldn't she die, I said to myself with evil glee, *if she knew I had a letter from her sweetie in my pocket!*

Phyllis left the post office disappointed. I didn't say a word. But I loved it!

The letter from Dewey Hurst turned out to be "plain vanilla"—a phrase I had coined to describe the unexciting. He said he was looking forward to seeing me at school.

I thought nothing of it. Just another musician looking for a friendly face along the road.

Mother and Dad must have helped me get admitted to North Central because the papers came and were all signed with no problem. My father paid the school bill, we loaded the car, and drove me to Minneapolis (after a farewell scene with my dog). My parents and I set up my room at school and the time came to kiss each other good-bye. I could see in their eyes how they loved me and would miss me.

I looked around at my new home and sighed. No longer little Aggie, the bed-ridden weakling, the African curio. I could start over now.

My rambunctious cousin Ruth (of the Irene-and-Ruth duo) walked in moments later.

"Cute," she reported, looking over my furnishings, "kind of cute."

Then down to business. "Hey Aggie. There's a social across town tonight for freshmen," she said. "Want to go?"

I agreed readily, and at the appointed hour we boarded an old streetcar. The moment we walked into the church foyer, ever-flamboyant Ruth began introducing me to her friends.

"This is my cousin Aggie Berg," she said, "but not my real cousin. My aunt and uncle found her in Africa."

I was horrified.

The students looked at me in wonder and I felt sick. Then, before I had a chance to defend myself, Ruth pointed to a group of students and I recognized Dewey Hurst among them. "See those boys over there?" Apparently Ruth did not know of Irene's matchmaking schemes, for she said, "They're some of the top-notchers. Don't go making a play for one of them; they wouldn't have anything to do with you."

Dewey, I was delighted to see, began making his way toward us. Ruth smiled happily, but wouldn't you know ... Dewey looked past Ruth and spoke to me.

"Welcome to North Central," he said, his eyes dancing. "Could I take you home tonight?"

"Sure," I responded.

Later Ruth shook her head and said, "Oh, well. It'll never last between you two."

On my first Sunday there I stayed home from Sunday school and read the paper. I was completely on my own and wanted to see how it felt. In fact, I resisted any kind of restraint I could. We were supposed to wear black uniforms with white collars but I perfected the art of wearing whatever I chose. My uniform, it seems, was always at the cleaners.

The horror of being "the girl the Bergs found in Africa" soon faded as Dewey filled up my social calendar. To Dewey, apparently my background was immaterial. He never questioned me, never quizzed me about the likelihood of epilepsy in my ancestry or the seven ways to serve hippopotamus to dinner guests. Two weeks after our first date, I went out with another boy on campus. Dewey objected.

"I hope you will not do that to me again."

"Do what?" I asked, surprised. "What'd I do?"

"You went out with another guy!"

"You gotta be kidding," I replied. "I might go out with a hundred more guys!"

"No. No, you won't," Dewey answered prophetically, and over the next weeks he proved his point. At North Central Bible College, freshmen were only allowed one date every other week. Dewey booked me for my next available evening, and before that evening was over he had suggested a really great idea for going to the State Fair the *next* evening, two weeks away. And so it went.

True to Dewey's prophecy, I never again went out with anyone else.

Dewey was an admirable gentleman, always polite, quick to the door, careful to walk on the lady's right side. I was charmed, and then enchanted, and then in love with this skinny young man.

It was wonderful to have somebody regard me the way Dewey Hurst did. He considered me petite and witty and pretty—and a fantastic conversationalist. He saw me as rooted in the faith. He loved my singing voice. One evening Dewey put all this together by proposing to me. I was so afraid I hadn't heard him right that I talked a blue streak. Dewey *couldn't* really be proposing. After all, I had this complicated past and—

"I don't care where you came from," he replied warmly. "And I don't care who your parents were. I love you."

It was a novel concept for me, to be loved just because I was me. I had been loved much of my life, but I always felt that I had been loved because I was helpless, or because I was stranded and orphaned, or because I was sickly.

Dewey Hurst cut through all of those perceptions. He just loved me. He loved me for who I was—not where I came from or by what route.

I was terrified when it came time to meet Dewey's parents. His mother's name was Frieda. She was German and had been a schoolteacher. They lived in Superior, Wisconsin, where Dewey's father pastored the Assemblies of God church.

But everything went well. I could sense that they were wonderful people and that in time I would develop a very special relationship with both of them.

We were married and I had never been happier. Dewey

taught me to love the Lord, more ful heartedly than ever before. His faith, so solidified my own. And the need to rebel— own sake—faded. Dewey even helped me fir the parts of my life that still troubled me, questions about my mother and family, th block our happiness.

But the greatest thrill of becoming Mrs. D. V. the vivid realization that I would never be alone hours upon hours of forced solitude were behin ever.

Or so I believed.

7

Cursed

Ah, when to the heart of man
     Was it ever less than a treason
To go with the drift of things,
     To yield with a grace to reason,
And bow and accept the end
     Of a love or a season?

—Robert Frost

A young California couple found badly needed jobs in a war plant. Rather than spend their income on a babysitter, they locked their four-year-old daughter and two-year-old son in their trailer house each morning and went off to work. The girl was given instructions to eat food off the kitchen counter when she got hungry, and to give the baby his bottle when he cried.

The horrified neighbors waited a few weeks, then called authorities. Health Department officials investigated and found the place a shambles. The children were unkempt and in danger of infection. The state filed suit against the parents and secured custody of the children, then turned them over to the father's parents.

Grandma and Grandpa Tucker were members of my father's church in Sioux Falls, where Grandpa Tucker served on the board of deacons. They were good people, but hardly able to cope with two little children, so eventually they decided to concentrate on helping the two-year-old boy and asked Dewey and me to foster Diane. I took one look at the six-year-old with the long blonde hair, the big blue eyes, and all those freckles. I glanced at Dewey and knew he was feeling the same way I felt.

Dewey had accepted an offer to teach in North Central Bible College, our Alma Mater, in Minneapolis. We agreed to take her with us when we went, which is how Diane came into our lives. From the first she made us her own. When we enrolled her in school, the registrar asked her name. Before either Dewey or I could respond, she reported, "My name is Diane Hurst." Both Dewey and I held our peace.

There were problems, however. She awoke nearly every night screaming. I sat on her bed, holding her head in my arms and smoothing her tousled hair and identifying with her. Diane was a replica of myself—not quite orphaned, not yet quite at peace with her identity. I wept with her, knowing precisely how painful it could be. She was my little Aina.

Diane's mother, Martha, had not forgotten her. She knew the law, and she realized that Diane could be adopted legally if she received no communication or support from her natural parents for more than a year. Her mother waited eleven months, then sent a ten-dollar bill with a short note.

Money was tight for Dewey and me in our new home in Minnesota but we found it hard not to shower Diane with toys and games. She was not only thoroughly lovable, she desperately needed to be shown such tangible love.

It was natural, then, that Dewey and I wanted to finalize adoption. But it would take the cooperation of Diane's grandparents, Grandma and Grandpa Tucker, since they had been given legal custody of Diane by the California courts. The Tuckers, though, were reluctant, even though Diane's mother had been divorced by now, and Diane's alcoholic father had been declared an unfit father by the courts. But whenever the Tuckers broached with Diane's mother the subject of giving up her daughter, Martha cried—and the Tuckers weakened.

Each time Grandma Tucker called with the latest news, I flashed back to those terrible trips to the Canadian border, when I was so fearful of losing my parents. Now the tables were turned, and I was fearful of losing my daughter.

Then, it was almost Christmas. The apartment was festive as Dewey and Diane and I packed all the Christmas presents for the holiday trip to Sioux Falls to visit my parents who were calling themselves Grandma and Grandpa Berg . . . and not only because of Diane. . . .

I was pregnant!

Diane had been living on a constant high ever since she learned the news. She loved to touch my tummy and remind the Lord that she was going to "get a new baby." Ours was going to be one rich family.

Then one evening the phone rang. Dewey answered and told me the news. Grandma Tucker's voice had been cold on the line.

"Martha wants the children back," she'd said, "and she has a court order to get them back. So as soon as you can get Diane here, we'll appreciate it."

In a flash of anger and emotion, hot tears filled my eyes and my throat constricted. I had never really believed it would happen. I always thought everything would work out—that Diane would be with us forever.

I was wrong. We knew that we had no money for a long legal battle and besides, our attorney had early on advised us without reservation that we would lose in court. We decided not to tell Diane until we were on our way to Sioux Falls. The father of my cousin-friends Irene and Ruth had made Diane a doll house, which she begged us to take along on the trip. We had refused—it was too bulky—but now we told her we could manage it. We loaded up her dolly and her buggy as well, knowing we would not unload them back in Minneapolis again.

On the road, Diane chattered happily about seeing Grandma and Grandpa Berg, about Christmas, about everything. When she finally paused, Dewey and I began the agonizing speech. After Christmas Eve, we said, after the presents and after Grandma and Grandpa Berg and after fun and food, she would be going back to Grandma Tucker's house.

Diane began to cry. There was nothing we could say. It was the worst misery.

On Christmas Day, we took Diane and all of her toys and clothes over to the Tucker residence.

It would have been painful enough just to leave everything—but Grandma Tucker, steeling herself for the ugly task, refused it.

"She can't have all this stuff," she snapped.

I looked at the woman, incredulous.

"Well, she's going to have the doll!" I replied hotly. "We're not going to take *everything* away from her!"

When we walked away, Diane was screaming.

"Mama! Will I ever see you again? How long are they going to keep me? Mama!"

I could not look back. Had I done so even once, I would have kidnapped her and fled.

It was death to drive back to Minneapolis without our child. Dewey and I talked in somber tones, wondering if we would ever try to adopt again.

"Do you think God will ever give us another chance?" I asked Dewey.

He sighed heavily and squinted at the highway.

Our lawyer advised us to hire a private detective to check on Diane's care. If he could document any instances of physical abuse, we might have a case for rescuing her.

As it turned out, Diane would suffer every kind of abuse but physical.

For weeks I was sick. Every time the news came on my ears perked up, hoping against hope that I wouldn't hear some horror story about my sweet little girl. Friends tried to comfort me by reminding me that I was pregnant—"Oh, Aggie," they often said, "you can always adopt another child."

But there would never be another Diane.

Only someone as remarkable and absorbing as Diane could have snapped me out of my mourning.

She called herself Gigi.

71

8

Fears and Farewells

It is a melancholy of mine own, compounded of many simples, extracted from many objects, and indeed the sundry contemplation of my travels, which, by often rumination, wraps me in a most humorous sadness.
— William Shakespeare

When she was born we named her Jayne Renee, but she resolutely called herself Gigi from the time she could talk. And talk she did. At the age of one year she was speaking in sentences and could hold the beginnings of conversation.

She had curly brown hair and big brown eyes, and she brightened the campus of North Central Bible College, where Dewey was teaching, as no academic luminary ever had. Perhaps best of all, she was ours—ours in such a way that no one could ever take her away from us. I praised God as I held her for the first time, touching her perfect little fingers and toes. *She's mine,* I said to myself again and again. *She's all mine.*

We moved to Springfield, Missouri, the day before Gigi's second birthday. There, Dewey had accepted a position as workers training director in the Sunday School Department at Assemblies of God headquarters.

We had been in Springfield only a few weeks when Dewey was sent out on the road for six weeks of meetings.

My life abruptly stopped—and started again, in a new, unhappy direction.

The isolation was exactly what I thought I would never have to face again. And now, in a new place, far from people I knew, I was scared. I found that I was full of fears, irrational, suffocating fears. I sat alone in our very small rented house, five blocks from Dewey's office, and the fears crept in on me. I was afraid of sounds and afraid of thoughts. Daylight was no help. I could not bring myself to walk down the street. And nighttime destroyed me. I sat alone with Gigi, my eyes darting around the room, for six weeks, the entire time that Dewey was away. In my mind I could hear the babysitters of my childhood: "All those Africans are going to come get you! . . . Your mean dad from Sweden is going to kidnap you!" Then I re-ran the scenes from Diane's nightmarish experience and grew even more fearful. They were absurd fears—and all the more fearsome because of their absurdity. Only as dawn began to break would my exhausted body finally give in to sleep.

It was into this atmosphere that our second child, our lovely baby boy, Rick, was born. Dewey had to leave again the next day. I was all alone the day I brought Rick home to that tiny house. I put his bassinet in the living room while Gigi slept on a rollaway bed in the dining area. The walls, already close, closed in even more.

I needed a healing from fear.

About a year later in the midst of a ferocious electrical storm a healing did come. On this night (Dewey was away again), one of the most ghastly electrical storms in the history of Springfield, Missouri, was raging through. Huge balls of fire exploded in the sky. Thunder rocked the earth.

Gigi and Rick both came screaming in from their bedroom. They jumped into bed with me and clung to me tenaciously. I was crying and shaking even before they awoke; now I was paralyzed with fear. My mind was whirling, my heart crying out for peace.

In that instant, a verse of Scripture raced through my head. I reached over to the nightstand and grabbed my Bible.

"I will lay me down and sleep in peace," I read aloud from the Psalms.

There it was.

"God," I prayed in desperation, "we ask You to deliver all three of us from this fear. Please send Your guardian angel to the front and the back of this house and give us perfect peace."

I can't recall setting the Bible back on the nightstand. Instantaneously, all three of us fell asleep.

The phone rang early the next morning. A neighbor was frantic, calling to see if we were all right and I was able truthfully, incredibly, to say that we were.

That morning the children and I took a walk. Lightning had struck right in the neighborhood. Trees had been felled all around our house. Pieces of houses and furniture and cars were scattered throughout Springfield. Electricity was off in most of the city.

We had slept through it all.

God had completely healed me of fear.

Later, however, there was another, deeper healing that was still required. Self-pity.

With my fears behind me, I could see my situation clearly—and I began to loathe what I saw. I was stuck in a tiny house in the middle of the Ozarks with only a two-year-old and a six-year-old to talk to. I could seldom get out; I had no car. My husband was often not home, so here I was, eating peanut butter sandwiches.

I felt sorry for myself, and the notion fed on itself. There were plenty of other wives of headquarters staff members with whom I could have socialized, had I made the effort—but to do that would have cheated me out of my self-pity, something I was not willing to give up.

The illness of the mind soon seeped into the body, and my joints slowly began to seize up. Movement became uncomfortable, and then painful, and finally almost impossible. Years after my African childhood, the strange symptoms of the rickets I'd suffered began trying to resurface. My right ankle began to bend in again as it had before, another flashback of my past. I took to moving around the house on a four-wheeled kitchen stool, groaning and moaning. Frequent trips to the doctor failed to accomplish anything.

Finally one day, the doctor grew exasperated with me. He wagged his finger angrily in my face and spoke harsh truth.

"Young lady," he said, "if you don't turn your self-pity around, you're not only going to have acute arthritis, you're going to leave your kids without a mother. Now you go home and you think about that!"

I was furious. I hobbled out of his office defiantly and cried all the way home, burning with anger. I sulked at home, but his words kept poking at me. I began thinking about my thought pattern of feeling sorry for myself.

Dewey was determined not to give in to my sullen self-centeredness and he told me why: He had watched his father spend a lifetime waiting on his mother. "I'm convinced that she failed to hold her own," Dewey said, "because Dad never challenged her. That pattern isn't going to repeat, Aggie."

Of course I knew what Dewey was talking about. Gentleman that he was, he didn't remind me how I sarcastically wished him well with his travels, his steak dinners and posh hotels. Or hung up in anger when he called me from the road. I pouted over my dust-laden floors, pouted because I couldn't operate a vacuum cleaner because of my aching bones. I sulked when I thought about getting up and facing the children and only the children—again, day after day.

My thought patterns were choking me. The doctor, I suddenly realized, was right. So was my husband. I had to think about things differently, get a healthier perspective.

When I awoke the next morning, I said, "Praise the Lord! It's Thursday! I have two healthy children!"

I looked at my still, silent vacuum cleaner and chuckled. I was hurting too badly to vacuum the floors—most women would be envious of me! And if my floor was a little dirty when anybody came over, they'd understand. If they didn't then they weren't worth worrying about in the first place.

One by one, I replaced old negative thoughts with positive ones—years before positive thinking was fashionable.

I began to relish the times Dewey was home, never again wasting a moment on self-pity or sarcasm. Our relationship began to deepen day by day, and when he was away, we only grew fonder of each other.

My joints, slowly at first, but then more rapidly, began to ache less violently. In a few weeks, I was feeling wonderful, both physically and emotionally.

And for "dessert," Dewey presented me with a fully paid-off car. It was an old green Plymouth, and I immediately named her Shasta—because "she hasta have gas . . . she hasta be pushed . . . she hasta get a tune-up . . . she hasta start!" Soon everyone in town knew Shasta, from housewives to mechanics. A dear friend of the family made Shasta his special project, always seeing to it that she was in good running condition for me.

It was like parole to be able to pile my kids in that old car and take off. Month after month we had languished at home, unable to get around. Now we were mobile.

Gigi was nine when she was diagnosed as diabetic.

Once again Dewey's philosophy of challenging illness was put into practice. He did not allow us to treat Gigi as if she were ill, since in fact, the doctor explained, she was not. Diabetes is much like nearsightedness: the pancreas fails to produce insulin, in much the same way that a myopic eyeball fails to produce clear images. Instead of wearing glasses, Gigi had to inject insulin. Dewey and I practiced giving shots to an orange so we could help Gigi. After that she had to help herself—learn in time to give herself her shots, avoid sweets, eat simply. We would *not,* Dewey repeated, treat Gigi as an invalid.

But complications developed—not medical, but social and emotional.

The diabetes did take Gigi out of school day after day. Absences led to adjustment problems, and adjustment problems led to more absences. She was on the yearbook staff her junior year in high school and scheduled to be editor the next year, but her absences threatened to change all that.

One day we discovered that Gigi had been taking our VW and driving around town instead of driving herself to school. Eventually we had to have her tutored at home.

She was such a bright girl, so intelligent that the tutor had trouble grading her fairly. She didn't want to give Gigi straight A's and reinforce the impression that she could get by without working at it. But that was the fact: Gigi rarely had to work at it.

So it seemed to me all the more important that the children have a disciplined and consistent homelife.

I determined never to work, even when money was tight, because I had seen in Diane's life what absentee mothers can do to their children. Ironically, even on a single income, our family thrived. We never had luxury, but our needs were amply met.

My children have not been perfect. They have only been delightful. My mother watched with horror as I raised them. I determined to let them learn by experience rather than require certain behavior. As a result, they faithfully nurtured personal relationships with their heavenly Father—and they smother me with kisses and love and appreciation every time they see me. I had been embarrassed in school by not being allowed to see any films, even educational films. And when the rest of my generation was learning to dance, I was forbidden to participate. (I danced anyway, secretly.) Now, with children of my own, I swung the doors wide open. And they never embarrassed me.

As for the taboos, the things I wanted them to *want* to

avoid, I took an approach that must have seemed questionable to a lot of people. When Rick was a teenager Mother and I were chatting one evening when he walked into the room wanting permission to attend a rock concert downtown.

"Can I go?" he asked.

"I don't know, Rick," I replied. "Can you?"

"What do you mean by that?"

"I don't know anything about that show," I answered, "but what I've heard about it isn't too good. So I don't know if you can go or not. I can't live your Christian life for you, honey. If you can go and participate and enjoy it without it bothering your conscience, feel free. You're seventeen. I can't make these decisions for you anymore. Think about it, pray about it, then decide."

Rick left the room, irritated by the speech I had made. His grandmother shook her head.

"He'll go, Aggie," she said, "you know he'll go."

Twenty minutes later he walked back into the room, dressed and cologned. He kissed me good-bye and smiled broadly. "See ya later," he chuckled. "Pickin' up my girlfriend on the way."

I went on talking about other things—but I could see that Mother was horrified by what I had done.

"Aggie!" she finally said. "How can you just sit there and chatter on and on, like nothing is happening?"

I tried to explain, but it made no more of an impression on her than it had on Rick.

An hour later the front door opened. Rick and his girlfriend walked in and plunked down on the couch.

"That was the darndest fourteen bucks I ever spent," Rick said disconsolately. "That was the most horrible thing I've ever seen in my life. We got up and walked out."

I hugged him.

"But thanks," he said, "for letting me decide."

"Rick, if I could be a Christian for you, I would," I told him. "I'd be first in line if I could take your place, and Gigi's place. But I can't. You have to do it yourself."

Soon, I would find myself wishing the same thing—for my long lost brothers, and my sister, and Mr. David Flood.

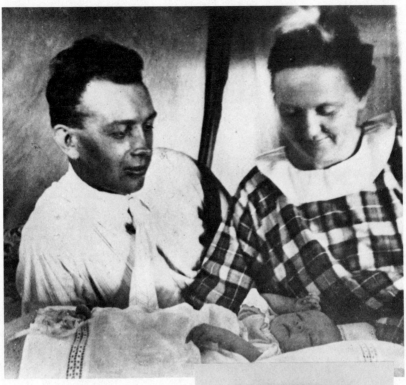

This is something of a "miracle" picture of me with Joel and Berta Erickson in the Congo, shortly after my father, David Flood, returned to Sweden. It was sent to Dewey many years later from someone in Sweden; he never learned who.

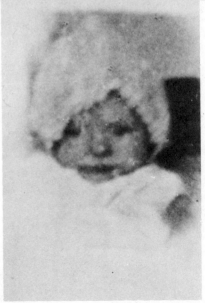

Here I'm in my brother David's baby clothes in Africa, 1923.

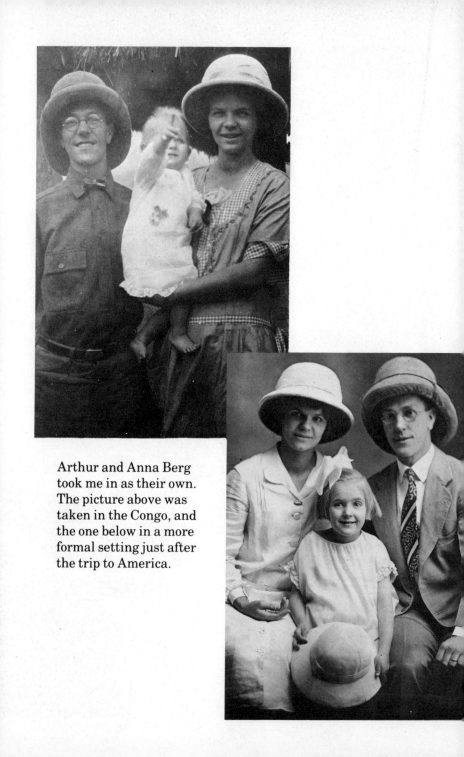

Arthur and Anna Berg
took me in as their own.
The picture above was
taken in the Congo, and
the one below in a more
formal setting just after
the trip to America.

A high school picture...

...and a more typically active high school scene.

July 7, 1944: Dewey and I marry...

...and enjoy life at home with Dottie.

(Above) The Bergs join the Hursts for Christmas.
African influence remained in evidence on the wall.

(Below) Dewey and I celebrate our twenty-fifth wedding
anniversary. Pictured with us are Darrel, Gigi, and Rick.

Here with Britt, the Swedish nurse-translator, I meet the African Kihabiro, who as a teenager carried me in a hammock on the three-day trek to the main station at Uvira when I was seventeen days old.

How awed I was to be able to pray at the grave of my mother, Svea Flood. I had found my roots at last.

9

Please Forward

Burnt child fire dreadeth.

—John Heywood

I always knew he was alive. I had been afraid of him since childhood, as my babysitters conjured up the ugly picture of a negligent faraway father. Then there was the mysterious letter, asking for sponsorship to America, which had been lost. And the letter from Aunt Signe, in Brazil, warning us about him.

But as I grew older I began to wonder about him and to dream that someday I would meet David Flood.

I developed a longing to visit Sweden. It was impossibly expensive, but perhaps in ten years, for our twenty-fifth wedding anniversary, we could make the magical journey.

Without our knowing it, God began setting in motion the details to make my dream come true.

Dewey and I tried to get in touch with David Flood. We wrote to an old Gothenburg address that had been given to us but the letter came back. Against logic, we wrote again but to no avail. We placed a call to the Philadelphia Church in Sweden. Did they have any idea of the whereabouts of David Flood? No. He was long gone.

I looked at the envelope of the latest letter, marked up by Swedish postal personnel. And then a simple idea occurred to me. I put the letter into a new envelope, addressed it, stamped it, and marked "Please Forward" on the outside. Then Dewey and I held the letter in our hands and prayed that God would put it into David Flood's hands.

Weeks later a note arrived, a scrap of paper torn from a notepad, and the message was handwritten in an unsteady scrawl:

"I would be happy to see you when you arrive in Sweden. David Flood."

I couldn't help crying.

"He can't even say 'Father,' can he?" I said to Dewey.

Dewey put his arms around me and promised that if ever we could find the money, we'd make our way to Sweden to visit David Flood. Was it possible, I wondered, that a visit to Sweden would provide some of the answers I had sought so long?

We had lived six years in a whirlwind. Then after almost ceaseless traveling for the Assemblies' Sunday School Department, Dewey was promoted to the directorship of the Radio Department. His travel schedule shrank dramatically, and we had a field day as a family, enjoying his presence as never before.

Springfield became great fun. We enjoyed meeting all the Assemblies leadership. The most notable of all—nothing less than a legend—was the irascible, irrepressible C.M. Ward, who preached weekly sermons on the *Revivaltime* radio broadcast for more than a quarter-century. It was Dewey's duty as head of the Radio Department to keep track of C.M.—no small chore. We spent a lot of time with C.M. and his wife, Dorothy, and grew to love them both. C.M.'s travel schedule resembled the one that Dewey had left behind, so Dot and I understood each other. I knew what she meant when she talked about weekends when "the king" came home!

Perhaps the most revered name in the entire Assemblies of God is the name of Thomas Zimmerman. Having served as the movement's top man for more than twenty-five years, the white-haired, bespectacled Zimmerman still inspires awe in many a preacher.

For a time, Tom and Elizabeth Zimmerman lived a few doors from us. C.W.H. Scott, another venerable dignitary of the movement, and his wife lived across the street. We three wives cared for each other's plants during trips and swapped rides when somebody's car was unavailable. I had been in the Zimmermans' home as a child, when my mother held revival meetings in their local church—and I sang. My mother had even sewn for the Zimmerman kids. They were wonderful people and I never felt intimidated by them.

One day, in the middle of a hot Ozark summer, I walked over to their house in my shorts—regular July attire for me. Elizabeth came to the door and her jaw dropped.

"Aggie, you shouldn't," she said. "Tom might come home and see you."

I wrinkled up my forehead and looked straight at her.

"Tom who?" I inquired. "I've been wearing shorts in front of God for *years!*"

It was also in Springfield that I finally was granted official U.S. citizenship, something I had wanted since childhood. I was legal at last! Our family partied after the court appearance.

We would move a final time, to the Seattle area. Dewey was offered the presidency of the Assemblies' Northwest College in Kirkland, Washington. It was a proud moment for both of us: Dewey would be the first Northwest president who had an earned degree.

But leaving the security of Springfield had its horrors for our children. Gigi in particular faced the problem. Her frequent absences from school, the social and psychological adjustments, had caused tension for her since she was nine. Now, just as things seemed to settle down for her, we announced in the spring of her junior year that we were moving to Kirkland, Washington. Gigi exploded.

"You're ruining my life!" she screamed. She stomped around and slammed doors and sulked over her food for days. One day she left the house unannounced and stayed out well after she should have been home, until finally she returned to a frantic family.

Rick's reaction was different. He resented the uprooting too. Rick was comfortable in Springfield. Our house was in a rural setting, complete with horse, dog, and cat (Rick's close friend, whom he called Elmer), and I'm sure he was sick at the thought of leaving them. But he never made a scene. Instead he kept his feelings inside.

In the final analysis, though, we did pack up our belongings, find homes for all the animals, and say teary farewells to our friends. Almost immediately the problems began to appear.

Gigi was enrolled in one of the typical, sophisticated West Coast suburban schools so different from simple little

Glendale High of Springfield, Missouri. Many of her teachers back in Springfield had been Baptist, Nazarene, or Assemblies of God. Here, life was "hip" and "slick" and Gigi was terrified. In her first week the girls in school demanded to know whether or not she was a virgin. We moved her over to Bellevue Christian where female students wore a uniform: white blouse, plaid skirt, and bobby socks.

Adolescence, diabetes, the moves, and second moves were rushing together in an emotional riptide. The day came after nearly a year in our new home when everything finally exploded. Gigi stayed home, claiming illness, and an argument began. Suddenly I realized she had locked herself in the bathroom. I banged on the door.

"Leave me alone! I know what I'm doing!" she shouted, threatening to overdose on insulin.

I dashed for the phone and called Dewey at the college. Dewey was scheduled to fly out of the state for a crucial speaking engagement. But he rushed home, assessed the situation quickly, and canceled his speaking date for a higher priority. He had never given in to Gigi's moods, always stressing the principle that her emotions were subject to *her,* not the other way around. This time it was no different.

Dewey let Gigi know how upset he was. He demanded that she come out of the bathroom and face his anger. When she did he removed his belt. Gigi's eyes grew wide. She was seventeen years old! A spanking was entirely out of the question. She was a senior in high school! Honestly!

No argument would dissuade Dewey. I had never seen him so upset, and yet it had an honest, all-out-in-the-open feel.

When it was all over, though, I could tell that Dewey

began to have doubts. When at last we were in bed that night, he spoke up.

"Maybe I was too hard," he said, his voice tight. "Maybe we've lost her. But what else was there to do?"

I had no answer.

That night we worried and wondered and prayed, but we could not sleep. The hours stretched out endlessly. Finally, as midnight struck, the door to our bedroom swung open.

Gigi ran to us and threw herself across the bed sobbing.

"Thank you, Daddy!" she said at last, when she was able to talk. "I needed that!"

The change was abrupt, and lasting. The move was completely accepted after that. Gigi was a new person. To this day she unashamedly points back to that experience as the moment she turned the emotional and spiritual corner.

Rick too came to a point of acceptance in the move. It was not with Gigi's bombastic style, but rather in his own low-key way. A few days after the spanking explosion, Rick confessed that he too was having problems adjusting. He hadn't said anything, he explained, because he didn't want to add to our troubles.

"Gigi has been such a stinker," he said, empathizing with us.

Perhaps Dewey and I failed to give Rick the attention he needed because our resources were so demanded with Gigi. The squeaky wheel does get the grease, and Rick was unwilling to squeak.

When word came one evening that Rick had cracked up the car on Interstate 5, we were upset. Rick was worried about his dad's reaction to the damage he had done to the car. But of course when Rick arrived, looking sheepish, Dewey rushed to him, embraced him, and made sure his son was all right.

10

Dreams Come True/False

There is a strength in the union even of very sorry men.
—Homer

Dewey and I could never have arranged such a voyage. When God does it, He does it right. We flew first class. When we stepped onto the plane, a flight attendant pinned a corsage on me. Henry Portin, a member of the college board who also was a professional photographer, snapped pictures for posterity. A Swede's first trip to Sweden—to meet her family for the first time! The crew members were thrilled. I was flying before we left the ground. I sat back in my seat and let the tears roll down my cheeks.

"All my life," I said to Dewey, "I felt like I was nothing. Yet here I am, a queen." I was unprepared for the dizzying sensation.

The plane landed at seven; we were in our hotel room by eight. Twenty minutes later we were called downstairs.

David Flood's sons had seen my letters and now all four men were in the lobby, anxious to meet "little Aina." How long it had been since anyone had called me by my Swedish name! My heart was pounding. Would they love me? Hate me? Had they come to stare, like so many people had done through the years? All the misgivings of my childhood swirled around in my stomach.

It was an incredible moment. As Dewey and I walked into that lobby, I came face-to-face with all four members of my imaginary family from childhood. All four were now standing together, and I recognized them as they came forward.

The second-oldest brother of my imagination had been a Casanova, outgoing and friendly, and his name had been "Joseph." Incredibly the first man, perhaps forty years old, to introduce himself said in excellent English, "Hello, Aina. I'm your brother Joseph." He gave me a big smile.

The third imaginary brother, the free-wheeling "Gene" of my childhood, grinned at me in real life. "I'm your brother Don," he said happily.

My imaginary Mama's boy "Steve" was a little shy; I went to him and hugged him. "I'm Bengt," he offered, blushing.

I hugged them all, weeping and laughing. But there was a fourth real-life brother, I knew. "Is that David?" I asked Joseph, indicating a man who was standing off a little way, alone, watching us. He was short, white-haired, disheveled, glassy-eyed, older than the rest, perhaps about fifty. As I moved slowly toward him, I could smell alcohol. *Oh, no, God,* I prayed silently, *this can't be David.*

"This," Joseph said uneasily, "is your brother David."

I looked at what appeared to be a beaten man, hardly able to stand up, a wrecked human spirit. I wanted to run. I wanted to forget I had ever seen him. But Jesus spoke to me at that moment: "What would *I* do now?" He asked me.

And of course I knew. I took David in my arms and hugged him hard. We both began sobbing.

"David, I love you," I whispered in his ear. "I've waited more than forty years to hold you in my arms, and I do love you." I took his face in my hands and looked at him squarely. "I've dreamed about you. You're my brother."

David must have *felt* something warm coming from me but he certainly didn't seem to be understanding. He started talking to me in Swedish. I looked around in bewilderment at my other brothers, all of whom had spoken in excellent English. Joseph explained that David couldn't understand a word I was saying. Growing up in the streets of Stockholm, he had not learned English as a second language as most Swedish children do. Joseph and my other brothers roared with laughter, and then so did David and I.

Suddenly our meeting exploded into a festive reunion and I realized that I'd neglected poor Dewey. The introductions began all over again. There were millions of bits of history to learn on both sides of the Atlantic. We all talked over one another and then repeated ourselves and laughed and chattered and did it all over again. Don interpreted for David and Dewey and me, further increasing the noise level. We turned the hotel lobby into a circus, noisy and hilarious and happy. I especially liked having them call me "Aina." Their Swedish accents turned the name into something smooth and lovely.

Later, we moved the celebration to Joseph's apartment, north of Stockholm. I learned a lot about my imaginary-brothers-turned-real. Joseph, the best-looking brother, was on his third common-law marriage. A successful supplier of fuel to tankers, Joseph was enamored of my American heritage. He was excited to learn that our house had three bedrooms and that we drove a Buick Electra.

Don was a good-hearted man, always quick to serve, always on the lookout to make sure everyone was taken care of. He too was financially successful, an executive with Texaco.

Bengt was kind and gentle and calm in every situation. He ran a fresh produce business, supplying groceries all over the Stockholm area.

David continued to be a shock. I had imagined him as dark, handsome, tall, ready for all sorts of fun. But now I was confronting the real David, almost the exact opposite. This David was only slightly more than five feet tall, with a snow-white crew cut. He was broken, distant. Having lived with the aging twin aunt and uncle out in the rural country for so many years, he was not inclined to hilarity. His bitterness had eaten away at his heart, and alcohol was working on the rest.

All of them were chain-smokers. All but David had wives, but not one of them was legally married. I learned their "wives'" names but throughout the early, exhilarating conversations with my brothers, I kept hearing an unfamiliar name—Ingrid. Finally, puzzled, I asked them who in the world Ingrid was.

"Our sister," Don replied evenly.

I looked at them in astonishment. "We have a sister?"
They were not enthusiastic. "Yes."

"Where is she?" I demanded eagerly.

"Oh, too far away."

"Nothing is too far. Where is she?"

"Gothenburg."

"Do you have a phone number?"

It was David, I noted, who had the number memorized. The other three brothers shifted uneasily as I dialed.

The phone rang in Gothenburg, and a woman answered.

"This is your big sister Aina," I said cheerfully.

I heard the phone clatter to the floor. Ingrid must have fainted.

Then a man came on the line. "Who is this?"

I told him who I was and that I hoped he and Ingrid would meet us at Joseph's place. Ingrid came on the line again and began yammering excitedly. My brothers gathered around me and started yelling directions in Swedish to her.

We learned later that when Ingrid hung up she grabbed a toothbrush, a nightgown, and her purse, and she and her husband dashed out the door. It was only after they had been on the road a couple of hours that they realized their children were still at school, forgotten in all the excitement. They stopped and called back to the house.

It became clear as we talked about Ingrid, while waiting for her, that she had never been close to her brothers. Like David, she was full of bitterness toward her father and also toward the brothers because they had never sought her out. Only David had stayed in touch with her. In her teen years, I learned, Ingrid had met David Flood by accident on a downtown Stockholm avenue. She told him she was getting married and he pleasantly asked for the wedding date. He would attend, he promised, and bring her a nice gift. Uncharacteristically, he hugged her good-bye. She sent the invitation; he did not show up. He had never responded. She had never seen him again.

The moment Ingrid arrived at Joseph's apartment we fell into each other's arms and began sobbing. "This is an answer to prayer," Ingrid said through her profuse tears. "I really have a big sister."

I held her away from me and just *looked* at her. I believe I could have picked her out of a huge crowd. She was tiny, even next to me. We wore our hair the same way, we were wearing similar dresses, we made the same funny faces, and even talked alike—rarely finishing a sentence before going on to the next. Dewey watched us talk for a few moments and began roaring with laughter, unable to comprehend how we could possibly be communicating.

Again we had huge amounts of ground to cover. I knew nothing about her, she knew nothing about me. Ingrid even knew very little about her brothers and I was able to act as a catalyst for all of the family members to learn about one another.

Four hours after they arrived, Ingrid and her husband had to leave. But we arranged for them to return a few days later, the last day Dewey and I would be spending in Sweden.

Then, I determined secretly, we would get this family together—with its father.

11

Tarnished Name

Heaven gives its glimpses only to those
Not in position to look too close.

—Robert Frost

There were strange, unexpected twists to life in this
world of the past.

Dewey and I brought my four brothers to the Philadelphia Church on the following Sunday morning. Dewey had
been scheduled as the morning's special speaker and sat on
the platform. He told me, after the service, that he had advised the pastor that the Flood brothers were in atten-
dance. The pastor's face had darkened and he firmly
advised Dewey not to recognize them from the pulpit.
David Flood's memory was a sour one among the church
folk.

My brothers at first resisted the notion of a visit to our

105

father and Ingrid wouldn't consider it at all. Papa was bed-ridden and very, very sick, they noted. But the real reason, I was sure, was a family split by ugly bitterness. Most of the children hardly knew David Flood. In fact, until I arrived from America, they had not known that their father had once been a missionary. It wouldn't have mattered. Joseph loathed his father. Don ignored him. Ingrid was angry with him. David, more his father's clone than any of the others, could hardly talk about the man, and strictly refused to discuss Africa. Only Bengt, the baby of the family, who had never known his father's crimes, faithfully visited the old man.

I pressed the issue anyway. I was not going to leave Sweden without meeting David Flood. Reluctantly, my brothers agreed to take me for a visit.

Before we left Joseph's apartment, they issued a warning. I had often talked about my faith since my arrival. (Don found it funny, and reminded the bunch of us repeatedly that Aina could just say a prayer and God would give us "any old thing we want!") Now they advised me that I could never get away with talk about spiritual things if our father were there. Whenever he hears the name of God, they reported, he flies into a rage.

I sat silent, wondering if I could keep such a corrupt trust.

We arrived at a plain little apartment building in a lower-class section of Stockholm. At the top of the stairs was a door, and on the door a tarnished brass nameplate. I leaned down and looked at the nameplate more closely. It was grimy where the letters had been engraved, years before. The smooth surface, once shiny, was now greenish. But vaguely, beyond the smudgy surface, I could see myself in it, my face transposed over his name.

I was about to meet the man who had given me life. "O God," I said softly, gulping back the tears. "Am I finally here? Is this my home?"

I rang the bell. It seemed like an eternity as we stood there in the hallway. My breath caught. It was as if everything were caught in a great warp of time, and nothing would ever move again.

And then, the odd, expectant moment passed.

The door swung open. A fat Swedish woman stood there; she spoke briefly with Joseph and then, smiling broadly and talking rapidly in Swedish, she let us in. Dewey squeezed my hand and I squeezed back. This would be Martina. She had taken care of David Flood for twenty years and for that I was grateful. The room though was squalid except for many oil paintings on the walls. Liquor bottles lined every window sill, and dust lined every liquor bottle. A table was covered with more bottles. In the far corner—a small, wrinkled old man lay in a rumpled bed, his head turned away. Above his head, oddly, hung a canvas, partially painted, and nearby were color tubes and brushes.

David Flood.

Diabetes and a stroke had confined this 73-year-old man to this apartment for three years.

As my brothers and Dewey and I entered, David Flood turned slightly toward us. His cheeks were sunken, he was in need of a shave. His failing eyes, clouded by cataracts, were sunken into a wrinkled face. His short white hair had grown just enough to be unkempt.

Bengt touched him and said, in English, "Papa, Aina's here." Slowly, he turned toward me. I took his hand.

"Papa?" I said.

He began to weep; the corners of his mouth were turned down so by the stroke that he could hardly form words.

"Aina," he said, wringing out the word. Then: "I never meant to give you away."

I cried with him. I could hear my brothers sniffling behind me. "It's all right, Papa," I said softly, taking him in my arms and holding him like a baby. "God took care of me."

He stiffened suddenly. The tears stopped.

"God forgot all of us," he spat. "Our lives have been like this because of Him. I was in Africa all that time, and only one little boy . . . And then I lost your mother. . . ."

He turned his face back toward the wall.

I turned to Martina and asked for a clean washcloth and with it I gently touched my father's face. His flesh was grimy, and tobacco stains ran the length of his chin, streaking down from the corners of his mouth like a tragic clown mask. I washed his face slowly, now fully realizing why God had allowed me to receive that mysterious Swedish magazine in the mail on the day of our departure from the States.

"Papa, I've got a little story to tell you," I told him quietly, "and it's a true one. You didn't go to Africa in vain. Mama didn't die in vain. The little boy you won to the Lord grew up to win that whole village to Jesus Christ. The one little seed you planted just kept growing and growing. Today there are six hundred African people serving the Lord, because you were faithful to the call of God in your life."

David Flood's eyes swung around again, slowly, until they met mine. They were hopeful eyes, longing to believe the story I was telling him, longing to have the turmoil of his life redeemed in some way.

"Papa, that story is well-known by now. It was written up in a magazine. We have a great God, Papa. He is placing six hundred stars in your crown in heaven today for the souls you've won through that one little boy."

I playfully slapped his cheek. "Papa, Jesus loves you! He has never hated you! Do you think if He hated the Flood family He would let me be here today, holding you like this?"

Now the tears began again. They seemed to me to be hopeful tears falling from hopeful eyes.

"Papa, don't you want to see Mama again someday?" I went on. "She loves you, just like God loved her. She gave her life and she's standing at those gates waiting for you."

The old man's body finally relaxed.

"Papa, won't you give your heart back to Jesus?"

Between sobs, my father prayed aloud.

"O God, first of all, thank You for bringing my Aina back to me. Forgive me for all my meanness, and forgive me for. . . ."

He began a long list. His heart was mending as he poured out a life-long agenda of sinfulness. When he finished, he was smiling brightly, a new man again.

I gathered up every empty liquor bottle and ordered my brothers to trash them. Then I took the ones that still had liquor in them and ordered everything flushed down the toilet.

"Are you kidding?" Joseph protested. "That's expensive stuff!"

"If you don't flush it," I threatened, "I'll toss it over the balcony and it will kill someone. Then we can all go to jail together! What's your choice?"

"Well," Joseph responded, shrugging, "I'll take it home with me."

"No, you won't," I replied. "I'm the big sister now."

I turned and looked at all of them. They grinned. They could live with it.

My father called me back to his bedside. "Sing to me, Aina," he begged. "Your mama had such a beautiful voice; she was a soloist at the Philadelphia Church. You sing to me."

I sang my favorite hymn, " 'Tis So Sweet to Trust in Jesus." Then I sang "His Name Is Wonderful." And when he asked for one more song, I sang him the old Swedish song "He the Pearly Gates Will Open," and I added a personalized final verse:

He the pearly gates will open
And Mama and Jesus will be standing there:
And as David Flood walks that last mile,
You will see them waiting with outstretched arms.

"Papa," I said when we were ready to leave, "you know now that your sins are forgiven—they're under the Blood. You are cleansed and you are whole. I'm going to be praying for your spirit, that you won't think negative things anymore."

His face fairly glowed as we left.

That week, as the fantastic vacation continued, my brothers and I visited our father often. We took little cakes and every evening was a party. Martina turned out to be a special addition to the evenings. In spite of their unmarried state, it was clear that she loved our father deeply.

Each evening, David Flood quizzed me about the Bergs, about America, about my childhood. It was as if he wanted to assure himself that I had been well cared for, that my life had actually taken a turn for the better when he left me in Uvira of the Belgian Congo four decades before.

I, on the other hand, wanted some memorabilia of my mother. I'd taken to calling our father "Papa" now even to myself, instead of calling him "David Flood." So I asked Papa if I could have a picture of Mother and he directed me to a box full of photograph albums and told me to take back as many pictures as I wanted.

The one quality of the apartment that seemed out of character was all the artwork. Papa, it turned out, was an artist, and a very good one, I thought. His oils hung all around the apartment, giving it a museum-like atmosphere.

His cataracts had made his work more difficult and when his stroke made him bedfast, Martina began laboriously suspending his canvasses over his bed. A right-handed painter, the stroke forced him to learn to work with his left hand, and his paintings were accomplished with boxer-like jabs of paint, awkward strokes that somehow still came out lovely.

We laughed and talked and sang—and sang often. Our favorite for that beautiful week was "The Green Green Grass of Home," which everyone knew and everyone loved to sing. I couldn't help but cry each time we began it.

One night as the song ended, Bengt began to weep.

"Ah, Papa," he said, struggling, "if you had just kept Aina, we would have stayed together. We could have had a happy family. A big sister would have done it."

My father nodded sadly and patted my head.

"I believe so," he said softly.

On our last day in Sweden, Ingrid came to the apartment for her first visit with Papa since that encounter on the street so many years before.

Papa sensed that Ingrid had not sought him out as I had. He did not cry when she arrived. He put his arm around her but he was not smiling when he said, "Welcome, welcome." He asked her where she was living, asked about her husband and children, made small talk. Papa kept a steely veneer all the time Ingrid was there. He could not let her penetrate it.

Ingrid left the apartment more bitter than ever.

It was the sad moment in a wonderful final day in Sweden. We all vowed to stay in touch, and Dewey and I flew away.

Indeed, we would be in touch very shortly.

My brother Don called me in Seattle after only a few weeks. Papa had taken a bad turn. The brothers wanted me to return. Papa wasn't going to last long.

But I had just undergone surgery and wouldn't be able to travel for many weeks.

"Tell Papa that I'm there with him," I urged Don. "Tell him that I'm praying for him, and that I love him."

Don called me faithfully every other week with the latest news. Papa continued to deteriorate. The years of tobacco, alcohol and diabetes had weakened his system, so that gangrene began to set in. Eventually came the news that doctors had amputated Papa's foot. Two weeks later they were forced to take his leg at the hip, trying to save his life. I wanted desperately to fly over to be with him but the doctor refused to give me permission. Finally Don called with the last word.

"Aina?"

"Yes."

"Papa's gone." Don broke and began to cry.

"Oh, no," I sighed.

"Yes, he's gone."

Martina had been with him in the final moments, along with Bengt and his wife, and Don.

"Did he die in peace?" I asked hopefully.

"Oh, yes," Don assured me.

I wanted to attend the funeral, but I was too weak. Joseph did not show up for it. Ingrid showed up and made a scene, talking loudly—and haughtily. Martina was heartbroken.

Later I would learn that David Flood, in his final days, had begun painting scenes of Africa. In his final hours, in delirium, he had begun speaking Swahili.

Before God took him home, He took him back to Africa. And very soon, God would bring Africa to me.

12

Graveside Picnic

He was outcast from life's feast.

—James Joyce

When, at long last, I was strong enough to travel again, Dewey and I returned to Sweden. We found that Martina visited his gravesite two days every week, always packing a picnic lunch, always sitting by the marker and talking to Papa as if he were alive.

On one trip to the cemetery, Ingrid agreed reluctantly to come along. Ingrid was aghast that Martina would devote herself to Papa's memory. She was even more disturbed when I decided to sit by the graveside with her.

"You're nuts, Aggie," she shot at me. "You're just plain nuts!"

"Ingrid, these visits mean so much to this dear old lady," I tried to explain. "She thinks she's with Papa. It's making her happy."

115

Ingrid stomped off to look at tombstones and smell flowers.

Martina had almost no English and I spoke almost no Swedish, yet somehow I knew she was telling Papa that I was there. When she indicated through gestures that I might like to talk to Papa myself, I decided to pray instead.

"Thank You, God, for saving Papa's soul before he died," I began. "Thank You for loving him so much."

Ingrid wandered back and began complaining about her father in English, declaring her hatred for him, and calling him so many ugly names that I had to wonder why she'd come here in the first place. I knelt at the grave, between his humble, weeping mistress and his hateful, ranting daughter, until I could take it no longer. I got up and walked over to Ingrid and pointed back to the tombstone.

"That happens to be the grave of our father," I said firmly, "and I want to see some respect."

She glared at me. "How can you call him a father?"

"Whether we like that fact or not," I replied, "he brought us into the world and he's our father whether he runs off and leaves us or not. The Bible tells us to honor our fathers—there's no option clause."

Ingrid only snorted. The decay that had consumed David Flood would take its toll on baby Ingrid.

On a subsequent trip to Sweden, I found myself driving through Stockholm with Ingrid and Don. We went out to supper, and we were feeling rather jolly on our way back. Don loved to tease me about my religion, although I suspected that he thought highly of my faith, so I was not surprised at his suggestion as we passed a tent meeting.

"As long as we have our saintly Christian older sister

with us tonight," he said with a sly smile, "don't you think we should all go to church?"

Which is how it happened that we all walked into the tent. I was feeling ornery myself, so as I led the group in, I asked the usher to take us to the very first row. I couldn't understand a word, and Don interpreted for me sporadically, adding his own commentary along the way.

The speaker was talking about how honored we all were to have a special guest in the audience that evening. "By golly," Don whispered, chuckling, "he found out you were here!"

"And if somebody will help her," the speaker continued, "she really must come up onto the platform so that we may get a glimpse of her."

Two ministers walked off the platform and stepped into the audience about three rows behind us. With great care, they helped a tiny elderly lady out of her seat and onto the platform. The entire audience stood, applauding her. When the ovation finally died and the congregation sat down, the minister spoke to the little lady:

"Signe Carlson, tell us what God's done for you lately."

My jaw dropped. I turned to Ingrid.

"Do you know who that is!"

"No, who?"

"That's our Aunt Signe!" I whispered, remembering the letter we'd received so many years ago from this South American missionary, warning us not to trust David Flood. "That's your mother's sister!" I said.

"Oh, God," Ingrid muttered, looking at the little old woman.

I turned to Don, on my other side, and asked if he knew who the tiny woman was. When he shook his head, I explained to him also that Signe was our aunt, the sister of both his mother, Cecelia, and my mother, Svea. Don only shrugged. "I've seen her on TV all week," he said. "I didn't know who she was."

As soon as the service was over, I pushed through the throngs around her, offending dozens of Swedes in the process. I asked her, "Do you know who we are?"

She frowned as she looked from face to face.

"No," she replied thoughtfully, "but I know I *should* know."

"Well, I am Svea Flood's daughter," I said. "I am Aina."

Signe began screaming my name, clutching at my arms and squeezing me. "Aina! Oh, Aina! My Aina!" She hugged me and rocked me and looked at me joyfully.

"And this is your other niece Ingrid," I finally was able to tell her, pointing to my half-sister. "She is Cecelia's daughter."

Signe enveloped Ingrid and wept even more freely. I introduced her to Don next and the 79-year-old woman became more enraptured by the moment. Without hesitation, she canceled her plans for the evening and the next day—to spend with this family so long unknown to her.

"Your mother was an angel," she told me again and again. "God only let her bless this earth for twenty-seven years, and then He took her home."

As we drove away the next evening, it occurred to me how incredible it was that we had wandered across Signe's path. "So," I said to my brother Don, "do you believe in God *now*?" He grinned like a child and half-shrugged.

Neither Don nor my other brothers made fun of my faith after that day.

13

"Don't Look for Me"

Past hope, past cure, past help!
—William Shakespeare

My sister, Ingrid, had two daughters, the younger of whom phoned our house in Kirkland one day with astonishing news.

"Aunt Aggie, you must come over here," she said breathlessly. "Something has happened to Mama! We can't find her!"

"What do you mean you can't find her?" I asked.

"We haven't seen her for two months!"

"Two months!" I replied. "And you're just calling me now?"

"We thought every day something would happen. We really need you, Aunt Aggie. We know you could find her."

I sat down and rubbed my forehead. I knew I couldn't

afford it. We had just returned from another long international trip and money was tight. But I found myself saying, "I'll see what I can do."

I knew there was nothing I could do but pray.

The next Monday morning the phone rang again. This time it was my old travel agent friend who had received a free ticket on an inaugural flight from Seattle to Stockholm.

"Aggie, this flight is only for commercial accounts," he explained. "So since you represent Northwest College, get yourself some business cards printed up, and go to Stockholm for free."

My business card said "Aggie Hurst, Public Relations, Northwest College," and I passed them out all over the place.

I flew to Gothenburg, Sweden, and moved into Ingrid's house where her husband and two daughters were still trying to figure out what had happened. I learned that Ingrid's office had been told to take no calls from her family.

With little to lose, I went to a pay phone, pinched my nose and pretended to be a United States telephone operator with a call for Ingrid from the States.

When Ingrid took the call, I had to confess who it was and that I was calling from nearby.

"How did you get here?" she asked.

"I hitchhiked; it was a horrible trip," I replied cheerfully. "Then I flew the rest of the way and my arms are killing me."

Ingrid did not laugh. "What are you doing here?"

"I got a free ticket to Sweden, so I decided to come see you. How about it if I come to see you tonight?"

"I've moved," she replied cryptically.

"Well, Ingrid, I want to see you, honey," I insisted. "I've

come an awful long way just to talk on the *phone*. I guess I should have written you or something first, but this free ticket just came up out of the blue."

"You're not with one of the girls, are you?" she asked suspiciously.

"No, I'm all alone," I replied. "I'm in a phone booth."

Ingrid was silent for a moment before advising me of her decision.

"I'll let you come if you will hail a cab and have the driver come into the phone booth to get instructions from me."

I agreed.

I found Ingrid in a studio apartment with a kitchenette and bath and little else. She had left behind a spacious three-bedroom apartment with two bathrooms in a lovely section of Gothenburg—a mansion by Swedish standards—with genuine treasures, beautiful oil paintings, bone china from London, crystal.

The story she told me was odd. Her husband had made good money in his gift shop, but he turned every penny back into the business, except when he saw a boat he liked, and he had a whole fleet by now. Ingrid had worked to pay the rent and household expenses and fill their home with nice furnishings.

But it all ended one February morning.

Ingrid got up three hours early every morning to make a pot of coffee and read the paper and ease herself awake. As she sat at the kitchen table that February morning, her husband crawled out of bed, looking every bit a rugged, unkempt outdoorsman. He walked out of the bedroom wearing an old pair of pants with no belt and an old ragged T-shirt. He slammed the door behind him without a word as he headed for the shop. Her younger daughter came out of her room, pushed a toothbrush around her mouth for a few seconds, pulled a comb through her hair, and went out of the door as her father had done, and headed for school.

Ingrid walked into her younger daughter's bedroom. It was a dump. She walked into the bathroom. Dirty towels lay in a heap.

Ingrid, you're nuts, she said to herself. *I'm not going to live this way anymore.*

She packed her suitcase, wrote a note, and walked out the door. The note simply said, "Don't look for me, I won't be back."

Nothing would sway her. She had no interest in scriptural mandates, she did not want to claim any of the goods in her house because that meant coming into contact with husband and children.

I began a campaign of prayer for her, one that has not yet shown much in results. Only a loving God can soothe such bitterness. And only a willing heart can allow God to do His work.

Ingrid insists that she is happy being alone. But she is really only on the run from happiness.

14

Return of the Chicken-Seller

O youth foregone, foregoing!
O dream unseen, unsought!
God give you joy of knowing
What life your death has bought.

—Brian Hooker

While I was still in Gothenburg, Dewey called from home. My trip to Sweden would overlap a trip he had scheduled to London, where he was to participate in a Pentecostal conference. We could meet in London and attend together a meeting that would be one of the most significant of my life.

And almost, *almost* we did not attend the meeting at all.

Dewey and I had attended several sessions of the conference and decided to pay hooky for the next one; the late summer day was just too beautiful to miss. We wandered around awhile, doing some sightseeing, and then returned to our hotel to prop our feet up for a bit. We found nothing but dead ends at the hotel, though. The air conditioner had died and the hotel maintenance people would need two hours to rescucitate it. There was nothing worth watching on TV. We decided to walk back to Royal Albert Hall (where the convention was being held) to find somebody we knew and have a cup of coffee.

As we stood outside the auditorium, we heard magnificent music. We stepped inside and stood in the back to listen to a Russian choir singing *a cappella*. The entire audience, numbering in the thousands, sat spellbound listening to the mingled harmonies.

We sat on the aisle in the back row because of our tardiness. My friend Betty Wannenmacher, secretary to the Assemblies' General Superintendent, Thomas Zimmerman, arranged special seating for each conference event. On one previous night, Betty kindly placed Dewey and me in the Queen's Box. However, on this night, because we were late, we found ourselves on common ground. As people came in we slipped a couple of seats over to make room for them. Then, as more people came in, we found ourselves in the middle of a long, long row, and unable to slip out easily.

When the choir finished, and we wanted to go have that cup of coffee, the chairman stood up and announced he would have "the distinct honor of introducing the Pentecostal leaders of several nations of the world." My heart stopped. There must have been five hundred men on and around the platform.

"Dewey!" I whispered frantically. "We're going to be here all night!"

Dewey pulled a pad of paper and a pencil out of his jacket pocket and I began to doodle.

The first nation was called, and a man stood up, spoke through an interpreter for a few seconds, and sat down. I paid no attention. The second nation was called, and the process was repeated. I still paid no attention.

Then the third nation was called.

"The superintendent of the Pentecostal church in the nation of Zaire...."

My head snapped up, and I squinted at the platform. Zaire was the name taken by the people of the Belgian Congo, the land of my birth, after they had won their independence years before. Instantly, I grew dizzy.

"Dewey, something's happening to me," I whispered. "I've got to talk to that man."

"I agree," he responded.

I sat listening to the short black man so far away on the platform.

"I am the superintendent of Zaire," the man began in French through an interpreter. "In Zaire, we have thirty-two mission stations. We have a one-hundred-twenty-bed hospital. We have many, many large schools. In Zaire, we have one hundred and ten thousand baptized believers. We have just this last year baptized ten thousand in water. God bless you."

His time was up. He sat down.

I was so eager to talk with that superintendent that the service seemed to stretch on forever, with countless introductions and testimonies. My body ached. I sat there, wishing I could get out of my seat, until finally I could.

Dewey pushed through the crowd ahead of me, intent on corralling the man until I could get to him. When I reached the platform, Dewey was standing next to him—the blackest man I had ever seen, with the bright yellow eyeballs so typical of people from his region. His name was Ruhigita Ndagora.

"Sir, I have only one question to ask you," I explained through the gracious missionary who was interpreting for us. "Could you have met a young missionary couple by the name of David and Svea Flood? They were on a mission station, and all I know about it is that it was high on a hill."

"Yes, madam," he replied, "it was Svea Flood who led me to Jesus Christ."

I looked at Dewey and back at the man. The story of my mother's one little convert spiraled through my head.

"And who are you?" he asked.

"I am Svea Flood's daughter. I was born on that mountaintop."

The man looked at me as if I were a phantom. Suddenly, tears ran from his eyes, as if they had been held back for years and years. He embraced me and began swaying with me, African style, sobbing from the depths of his soul. He rocked gently back and forth, crying more and more, as I rocked and cried with him.

"I've so often wondered," he cried, "whatever happened to that little white girl whose mother died for us." He stopped and took my face in his hands. "We want to give thanks," he said, looking deep into my eyes. "Thank you for letting your mother die so that we can live."

The great question of my life, "Why?", finally had an an-

wanted us to know one thing: she had never forgotten what she learned in our home. She was working, finishing high school, hoping to become a beautician.

It was the first word we had received from Diane since she had left our home. She had always planned to look us up, to seek us out, she said, only never had. I began to cry as Dewey told me how she looked. She was still more like a natural daughter than anyone would ever believe.

The encounter, brief as it was, gave us peace. To know that our precious little one, who had disappeared so many years ago, was safe and healthy—it gave us a rest we had never quite been able to attain.

And there was the happy day when Dewey and I ran into Ward Drake, my childhood friend and confidant from twenty-five years earlier, the boy who had crawled over the roof of our house to talk with me and share sweets with me when I was supposed to be resting. Ward had come to an Assemblies of God convention in Long Beach, California. He told us that he had settled in California. It was a delight to see him again, to meet his family, and introduce them to mine.

The reunions with my family have been, of course, the most precious to me. To meet my father, only six months before his death, was a great blessing. To meet my brothers David and Joseph and Don and Bengt and my sister, Ingrid, is an honor I could never have required of the Lord. To be led by God's divine hand to my Aunt Signe, and to the African man my mother had led to the Lord so many years before—these are reunions I will treasure.

There were many happy reunions too with my adoptive American parents, the Bergs. We were family in every way. I was their only child until Dewey and I were married; then he became their son. We never knew a rift. There was love, appreciation, and concern for each by all.

swer. A crowd was gathering around us, many people weeping.

"My colleagues and I are on our way to Stockholm," he told us, "for a convention at Philadelphia Church. We took this picture of your mother's grave to show the people there." He held out a photograph of the same grave marker I had seen in the Swedish magazine years before. "We just painted the cross on your mother's grave."

Dewey and I looked at the picture of the cross. It was fresh and white, with black lettering: Svea Flood, 1896–1923. My mother had become a legend among the people of the Philadelphia Church in Stockholm. She had gone out as a young mother to the distant jungles of Africa. She had given her life for the cause of Jesus Christ where she had won a single soul—the young African boy who brought chickens for sale. But through him, she had won thousands.

It was a moment of great satisfaction for me except for one sad element: The only people who had never learned to thank God for Svea Flood were those closest to her—a man named David Flood, and the unhappy, fragmented family he later created.

15

Reunion

It was surprising that Nature had gone tranquilly on with her golden process in the midst of so much devilment.
—Stephen Crane

God has granted me many reunions, for which I am grateful.

The day came when Dewey ran into our sweet, almost-adopted daughter Diane in front of a Chicago church where he had been speaking. Dewey called home to tell me about the meeting. Someone had reached around from behind him and covered his eyes with the typical "Guess who?" He turned around to see a smiling girl about seventeen years old.

"Hi, Dad," she beamed. "You're still just as handsome as ever."

Diane had been through a life of hell after she'd been forced to go back to her natural family, she said, but she

My mother and father eventually settled in Springfield, Missouri, where Mother Berg still lives today.

But there was one piece of the puzzle of my past that I knew would be especially important to me, my return to Africa. Dewey and I had planned the trip for months, saving money, writing people who could tell us about the villages we wanted to visit, marking maps, drawing up schedules, on and on.

Now, finally, my reunion with the continent of my birth was at hand. The sights and sounds, I knew, would not be altogether foreign. At times I had visited spots in America that had strangely reminded me of Africa. One road down a steep hill in Kirkland was like that. We drove it many times. The trees and heavy underbrush, wet from the rain, made me feel I was back in the Congo among my Swahili playmates.

Now, Dewey and I flew to Burundi, where we were to be met by a Swedish missionary named Erickson (no relation to the Joel Erickson of the 1920s) who was to drive us across the border into Zaire, and finally to Uvira, the main missionary outpost in the old colony, Belgian Congo, where my parents served. When we arrived at the filthy little airport in the town of Bujumbura, we were the only white people to be seen. But finally Erickson arrived, grabbed our luggage, and threw it into his Peugeot trunk, which he hooked with an aging wire. There was no lock.

Once we were on our way, Erickson introduced himself and we went through the typical pleasantries.

"Now," he sighed, "I've got to do some shopping before I go home."

We were heading for the border of Zaire, so Erickson wanted to purchase a few things that were available only here in Burundi. Before he got out of the car, he reached into a secret cache in the upholstery of the front seat and pulled out several pieces of paper money. He had hidden a supply of cash from several different nearby countries—a practical, unofficial subterfuge for any African travel. Erickson bought a case of soda with the cryptic comment that we'd "need this later."

We drove for hours to the border of Burundi, and for hours inside Zaire. The roads grew from horrible to more horrible, never better than a single lane, full of craters and boulders. We were thrown all over the seats of the Peugeot. There had been no road maintenance since the uprising of more than a decade before.

But finally we arrived in Uvira, the outpost where I had been turned over to Joel and Bertha Erickson by my father—the place where they were poisoned, and Arthur and Anna Berg had rescued me. I was the guest of honor, African style. We were served thick coffee and crusty rolls full of little brown ants. To eat the rolls, we first knocked off the ants.

Then we went to the church, where more than a thousand Africans greeted us, clapping and cheering and waving flowers and leaves. I was given the prize—a live rooster—which was later cooked and served as dinner. There were greetings after greetings, which seemed to last for hours (I was reminded of the endless speeches at Albert Hall!).

Then I was asked to greet the people. No words seemed adequate. I could only thank these people humbly for their kindness. They had already done all the honors.

Missionary Erickson took Dewey and me out into the country, along a narrow path, and up a hill, to the place where I had lived until the missionaries died. A monument stood over their graves. Now, where that tragedy had struck so long ago, there stood a little chapel. There was going to be a wedding that day.

While we were at Uvira, the missionaries' shortwave radio began crackling with a message from someone at Massisi, a village hundreds of miles to the north. It carried the message of welcome from a man with whom apparently I had played as a child, although I confess I barely remembered him. He would have been my first "boyfriend." Back then they called him my "child boy." Today, he was a medical doctor.

I had never known the name of the village where I learned Swahili and played like a native African child with my friends. Massisi—far too remote to visit now (requiring a private flight plus at least three hours by Jeep)—would have to wait for some later, even more exotic journey.

The next day a Swedish nurse named Britt arrived in a VW ambulance from the hospital at another mission station. Her assignment was to take us to N'dolera, the village where I was born. Now we discovered why Erickson had bought all that soda pop. There was no running water beyond Uvira.

Roads now were almost nonexistent. Even fifty years after white men had penetrated this region, the Dark Continent remained dark. When we came to bridges our African helpers went ahead to jump up and down on them—just to make sure they would hold the hospital's Volkswagen ambulance.

We had stopped along the way to buy papaya from children at a pathside clearing when an old bearded barefoot man in a well-worn business suit approached Britt. Apparently word of our visit had gone ahead of us, for the old man pointed to me and ask Britt quietly, "Is that woman's name Agnes?"

Britt had not heard my American name. "No," she replied, "her name is Aina."

"It was Aina," the old man persisted, "but her foster parents changed it."

The old man reached into his pocket and pulled out an ancient, cracked photograph. He held it out to me: it was a picture of the Bergs and me.

He introduced himself with a happy smile. He had been our cook at Massisi. He was now a deacon in the church.

I embraced him, and we posed for a picture together. I gave him a much more recent photograph of the Bergs and me. And when we drove away from that papaya stand, I knew more assuredly than ever that God is at work in the details of our lives.

The "road" led up, continuously up the mountain, with the tires of our Volkswagen sometimes within inches of the precipice. When we arrived at N'dolera, six hundred Africans greeted us. They were laughing and crying out, "Aina . . . Aina!"

As we approached the village, I stood on the running board of the VW and waved and cried out, *"Santa sanna!"*—the traditional Swahili greeting. Everywhere people were waiting for me . . . throngs of children, their mothers and fathers, and the ancients of the village, gray-bearded or bald. They had built arches and overlaid them with flowers. I wondered if this weren't the greatest celebration this little village had ever assembled.

The pastor of the village church led me up the hill, with all the people following and talking excitedly. At the top of the hill was a flat place beneath a grove of trees. The pastor pointed to it and said, "This is where your house stood. This is where you were born."

Then the pastor turned and pointed, without a word, to a simple grave, framed in cement, a few paces away. I walked to it. Over it stood a single huge, beautiful palm tree, overlooking the entire valley.

The cross was so plain, so stark—just a wooden cross—and yet, to me, so beautiful. I could stand where my mother had stood, as she declared her faith in her own lovely way to the one small boy. And now I could know the harvest of the seed she had sown.

I knelt down, and the Africans backed away several paces. I began to pray from my heart, asking God to forgive me for ever questioning Him, for ever asking why. When I turned around, I saw tear-stained faces praising the Lord, clutching their Bibles—and all the answers were right there.

Out of the crowd hobbled a weak old African man in a red shirt and short khaki pants, led slowly by Britt. No one could say exactly how old he was, but his stubbly beard was almost pure white, and Britt explained that many had feared the old man would die before we got to N'dolera.

He had made the hammock-cradle and carried me to Uvira when I was less than a month old. This sickly old man, now near death, was as responsible as anyone for the life I had been granted. I had my picture taken with him, and he was beaming, basking in the glow of celebrity for this one brief and beautiful moment. The Africans cheered. For the remaining few days of his life, this man would be their hero.

The pastor led us back down the path to a stone church where there was a welcome feast of stewed chicken and rice. Later, during an official welcome service in the village church, the pastor opened the Scriptures and read, beginning with the words of Jesus:

"Except a corn of wheat fall into the ground and die, it abideth alone: but if it die, it bringeth forth much fruit" (John 12:24).

Then he read a single line from Psalm 126:5: "They that sow in tears shall reap in joy."

The service went on, but I was lost in my thoughts. As a deacon stood and recounted my story in Swahili, I was still back on those two promises. As I sat here, in the midst of my own heritage, I realized just how true both promises really are—and were. My mother, Svea Flood, had died, and tragically so; the corn of wheat had fallen into the ground. And yet there was this village full of fruit! All of the churches and schools! One hundred ten thousand baptized believers! I thought of the tears that were shed for her, the bitterness that had grown up around her memory—and unnecessarily. For here, in the very heart of the land that had taken her away from Papa, those tears had brought a harvest of joy.

I learned, that day, why the Africans insisted on calling me "flesh of our flesh." Somewhere beneath us, in the earth under N'dolera, was a part of me—the umbilical cord that was buried the day of my birth.

"You have always been one of us," the pastor said lovingly.

There was a completeness about this day, among the people of my birth. I felt that very wonderful and elusive quality of having come full-circle, almost as if this answered the last riddles of my life.

But no. There were just a few jigsaw pieces yet to fall out, yet to be replaced, in the life-puzzle.

16

The Broken Chain

We dance round in a ring and suppose,
But the Secret sits in the middle and knows.
—Robert Frost

In the bitter life of David Flood, history had a way of repeating itself in his family. But where Christ has been given control, history has a wonderful way of repeating itself as well.

It was delightfully appropriate for my first two grandchildren to be *chosen*—as I had been—by loving parents. Erich arrived not in a hospital but on a jet plane from Kansas City, at the age of six weeks. Our daughter Gigi and her husband, Darrell Hobson, adopted little Erich and our lives were changed forever.

Erich, of course, is the finest grandson anyone ever had. He is intelligent and witty. He considers any food a feast—

as long as it is eaten at Grandma's house. In the providence of God, Erich looks just like his adoptive mama, Gigi, and in fact has an identical birthmark on one leg. Erich calls his new mother "my Gigi-mama" and his new father "my Darrell-daddy."

Lindsay Ann, likewise, is of course the finest granddaughter anyone ever had. She arrived in April of 1980, also by jet, to bring equal joy into the lives of her parents and grandparents. She climbs and laughs and never stops. And she, according to God's grace and love, looks like Darrell.

Erich reports that he will never marry because he will never find anyone he loves as much as his mother and sister. Erich's heritage as a chosen child is a rich one already. One day as he and I were driving who-knows-where, Erich pulled one knee up and wrapped his arms around it and proceeded to explain how he was born.

"You know, Grandma, most little boys are brought by the stork," he reported. "But I wasn't. I came from God by United Airlines."

Erich's explanation of his birth continued: "I got on this big plane, and it took off and flew a long ways, and then when the plane landed, there was my Gigi-mama and my Darrell-daddy. They were waiting for me, because they chose me. And as soon as they saw me, that's when I was born. I was born in a pocket under my mama's heart."

How true. Some of us who are adopted have had that privilege—to be born in the pocket under Mama's heart. The day came when Erich understood his special relationship with me. Both of us, after all, were chosen.

Literally every day I have thanked God for His mercy in allowing me to break the chain of sin, despair, and bitterness in my past. I have inherited the faith, not the despair. I have been allowed to establish a Christian heritage for the children who would follow me, our children Gigi and Rick, and our grandchildren Erich and Lindsay.

But for years I prayed as much for my Swedish family as well. I prayed that somehow the miracle of Papa's late-in-life return to his salvation could happen likewise to his other sons and daughter.

God, of course, has His own timing. He has not worked on my timetable but he has given one beautiful glimmer of hope.

Her name is Agneta. She is my younger brother Bengt's daughter. When Agneta passed her twenty-first birthday she wanted to visit America; Dewey and I arranged for her to spend a couple of months with us. Agneta stepped off the phone in Seattle, a tall, impressive blonde. There was, however, a grayness to her blue eyes, and something heavy seemed to hover around her. She looked like a movie-version East German or Russian, flat and expressionless.

But one day she went with me to a meeting where I had been asked to give my testimony. Agneta had never heard my story before. In those moments, she heard how thoroughly God works in our lives, when we let Him!

In the weeks that followed, Agneta could see why our home was filled with love—a depth of love she had never known. And the day came when she asked me to lead her to Jesus!

It was a most glorious moment. Agneta's gray eyes turned to radiant blue. Her face fairly glowed. She was so bright and happy that when her father and mother flew to Florida to meet her some time later, Bengt could barely speak.

"You are beautiful!" he exclaimed. "What's Aunt Aina done to you? Taken you to some charm school?"

After Papa, Agneta was the first member of my family to accept Christ through the testimony of my tangled history. Hopefully she will not be the last.

Agneta Flood never returned to Sweden. She met a college student named Tom Heins while she was here, and they were married by Dewey in our living room. Agneta and Tom are planning to spend their lives in Christian service.

No finer way to break the chain of sin and despair.

And there was a final twist to God's plan for my life.

17

Not the Final Chapter

Forgive, O Lord, my little jokes
on Thee
And I'll forgive Thy great big one
on me.

—Robert Frost

Dewey had the opportunity to add full cancer coverage to the insurance policy carried by the college for its faculty and staff. He never guessed that I would be among the first to use it.

Cancer is always the final chapter. Except when God writes the book.

I had faced a variety of physical problems down through the years, from the earliest malaria attacks of my childhood to bouts with an ulcerated colon, from acute arthritis to a throat problem requiring surgery. But God saw me through every trial, and I remained happy and energetic.

There is one word, however, that cuts through life like a knife.

Cancer.

It is perhaps the most frightening word in the English language—deathly, dark, and mysterious. It has a slashing sound. It steals sleep, leaving only restlessness.

Cancer never made me sick (although the *treatments* for cancer certainly did!). I felt fine. But something inside me was wrong. I could feel something foreign, just under my ribs, on the right side. Day after day I poked at it until one day I noticed a change.

The mysterious something was growing. It was like a knob. Each evening I could sense more of it.

"Dewey, this doesn't feel normal, does it?"

There was no pain, no nausea, no exotic symptoms. There was only the questioning, and the dread.

This thing could be cancer.

The doctors probed and conferred in their mumbling way and decided that an operation was necessary. The family tried to be positive, tried not to frown with worry. I had been through surgery so many times before and everything had always come out fine!

On the fourth of March in 1980, Dewey and the family kissed me, and the orderlies wheeled me into surgery. We were finally going to get to the bottom of this thing. Whatever it was, we would soon know.

Surgery began early in the morning. When the surgeon finally emerged from his work, the news was bad.

A full day later, after each of the children and their spouses—and Dewey—had spent twenty-four hours adjusting to the truth, I came out of the anesthetic fully enough to be told. Dewey arrived with our pastor, Charles Anderson of Calvary Temple, and soon two nurses joined us without explaining their presence. I enjoyed all the company, but didn't understand its significance.

Eventually the doctor entered the room and began his cautious speech, while Dewey held my hand.

"I want to tell you about your surgery," he said. "I removed a large tumor, Aggie, the size of a grapefruit."

The obvious question came to my mind.

"Was it malignant?"

"Yes," he replied.

I had no response for that. It was one of those rare times when I lay silent, wondering what to say.

Someone prodded conversation again, and there was medical small talk. I asked a few peripheral questions, but none of us asked the big one.

Finally the doctor asked me if I had any other questions. He was wise in waiting; I would be ready for the answer if I asked the question myself.

"Did you get it all?"

I watched his face for the nonverbal answer to precede the verbal. His face was grim, so I knew. His voice was equally grim.

"No, I left about five percent," he replied. "I just couldn't get to it."

Silence filled the room again. I felt everyone waiting for me to explode into tears or hysteria or worse. But my God had prepared me for this moment. He had built up my faith over the years. He had seen me through too many trials. He had convinced me of my own value to Him, by keeping me in the palm of His hand. He had shown me how a horrible tragedy still has ultimate beauty—that God is always directing events, that He is always in control, that He never stops loving his children.

So I heard the doctor's words, but I failed to react as apparently he expected me to.

Instead, I smiled and took his hand.

"Doctor, don't we have a great God?" I asked him. "He let you, a man, take ninety-five percent and only left five percent for Himself!" The doctor tried to smile. So I added, "And I believe He will take care of it!"

The power of God rocked the room in that instant. The nurses who were there later testified that they had never felt anything like it. Dewey wept. The wonderful man who had taught his family to challenge every illness was now facing the greatest challenge of his lifetime. And the same was true for me. But as we talked, the unbending, unquestioning faith of my upbringing filled my heart. God had not salvaged me from the fevers and jungle of the Congo just to toss me into the trash. God had not given me life against all odds just to snatch it away for a lousy five percent!

The principles I had learned at my mother's knee, and in thousands of church services and Sunday school classes, and in the lyrics of the countless songs I had sung—even as much as I detested being subjected to them all—those principles now sprang to life. I had quit Sunday school the moment I got away from home, and yet now, facing the deepest crisis of my life, the corny little Sunday school lessons about faith proved to be the ones of real substance.

All the songs, the sermons, the hundreds of services, the lectures at home, and above all, the examples of faith and trust and consistency toward God came from beneath the surface of memory and did their work.

I rarely thought about the cancer after that. I determined to live every day just as freely and as happily as ever.

The real sickness, as it turned out, was yet to come.

The doctor advised that I submit to chemotherapy and allow medical science to do all it could toward the treatment of the final five percent. Dewey and I discussed it and agreed to follow their advice, deciding that we should allow science to do all it could as a part of our trust in God. We determined to maintain steady faith in God's handiwork and give Him the glory for every victory.

Chemotherapy is like death. You go to the hospital feeling fine, and within a few hours you are hopelessly ill. My reactions to the treatment were exactly like those of millions of others who have experienced it.

I entered the hospital and was immediately hooked up to an intravenous feeding apparatus, with the tiny needle poking into a vein and taped to my arm. From nine in the morning until nine in the evening, I was fed through my blood system and my system was flushed.

At nine in the evening, two nurses lugged a huge heavy bottle into the room and put it in the place of the feeding bottle. It contained two thousand cubic centimeters of platinum, the cancer-killing agent, which was circulated through my veins and arteries for another nine hours—until six the following morning.

When the bottle of platinum was about half empty, I began to get sick to my stomach. I vomited and vomited and vomited some more. I continued to vomit until the bottle had emptied all of its liquid platinum into my system, and I continued vomiting for several hours thereafter. My niece Agneta sat with me the first time; often, my son Rick and my son-in-law Darrell traded off at my side, each one holding the pan for me for an hour or two before letting the other one spell him.

After the platinum, I was hooked up to forty-five minutes' worth of adriamyacin to kill any bacteria that might have been swimming around in the platinum. Then it was back onto the feeding and flushing solution to build up my strength and cleanse my system. For the first several hours, strength was a distant dream. I lay there, completely weakened, unable to converse intelligently. The very mention of food made me sick all over again.

By nighttime, I was beginning to feel strong again. I slept the night away, and awoke feeling good, ready to go home. But once I got home, I could only bear to sit around for the first whole day.

I had nine such chemotherapy treatments, one each month for nine months. It only took two treatments for my hair to fall out.

I stood in front of the bathroom mirror and looked at myself—bald. It was not pretty. But I began to praise the Lord.

"God, You're really making me over," I sang out, "from the top of my head to the soles of my feet!"

And I pulled on a wig. I would wear it continuously for over a year—until after the final chemotherapy treatment of that series, when my hair finally grew back in.

Cancer pointed me to my unfinished business. I realized I would not live this earthly life forever, healing or no, and I had better make right some outstanding wrongs.

I had been bitter toward my brother-in-law Stig, whom my sister Ingrid had deserted years before. I felt Stig had been unfair with Ingrid, that in many ways she had been justified in feeling about him the way she did, if not in leaving him.

But Stig had moved; I couldn't locate him. So I began to pray that God would give me an opportunity to restore that broken relationship—somehow.

One day a car pulled up in front of our house in Kirkland. I had just finished cleaning. The vacuum cleaner was standing like a broken robot in the hallway; I was stationed at the kitchen sink with suds all over me when Stig arrived at the front door explaining that he had purchased one of those unlimited air passes from Eastern Airlines and decided to come to Seattle to see his long-lost sister-in-law.

I had my chance—even though I looked like a wreck. Within a few minutes I had settled my grudge, asking his forgiveness. Stig and I have been good friends ever since, although it has not been possible for him and Ingrid to get back together.

God began bringing other people to remembrance, compelling me to ask forgiveness. Having so often said exactly what I thought I had quite a bit of forgiveness to ask for— from a teacher here, a housewife there, a pastor far away, a businessperson close to home. I was surprised by the number, and by the variety, of my debts outstanding. But I set about to get my slate clean—and as far as I am able to tell, I did.

I had to. Cancer does that to you.

A year after the surgery, my doctor looked at me in amazement.

"Aggie," he declared, "only your faith and good attitude have brought you through."

There was no more evidence of cancer to be found in me.

Physical healing is never really the point. The point is what happens to a person's spirit, his character. Physical healing is just gravy; spiritual healing is the real meat and potatoes.

Furthermore, the most important result of my fight with cancer has not been limited to little old Aggie Hurst. My cancer could hardly be worth it if I were the only one to benefit. No, cancer opened doors of testimony as again and again, people in despair have asked me for help. And only because I have been in that same sort of despair, suspended between heaven and earth, stamped with the seemingly hopeless stamp of cancer, have I been able to point them to Jesus. ,

Many times, doctors or nurses or friends or relatives have asked me to talk to cancer patients, especially shortly after they learn their condition. One day a business associate of Dewey's asked me to call a woman named Maxine. She was dying of cancer at a nearby hospital.

"Maxine, you don't know me," I began, right on the phone, "but my name is Aggie Hurst, and I understand the valley you're going through. I've been in that valley myself. . . . But I want to tell you about a dear Friend of mine who went through it with me. He never left me alone, He was always right there beside me. His name is Jesus."

"Oh, really now—"

But, with gentleness I went on to describe how God had walked with me, and would do so with her. "He cares," I said. "I know that right now you don't think anybody cares—and you think, most of all, that God has forsaken you."

She was silent and I knew God had been using me to speak to this lady.

"When you walk through the valley," I went on, "God is always there. He is carrying you right now," I said. "Have you given yourself to Him?"

"Well," Maxine replied haltingly, "I'm a member of a church. And I've been confirmed."

"That's beautiful," I replied, "but there's just one more step: giving your heart to Jesus Christ. The Bible says,

'Ye must be born again.' Would you like to receive Him into your heart, Maxine, and be ready to meet Him after this life?"

She thought a moment before replying.

"Yes," she answered. "How do I do it?"

"It's so simple, it's hard to explain," I said to her. "So, just pretend I'm in the room with you, holding your hand, and I'll pray. You just repeat the words after me. And when I come to the part that says, 'Come into my heart, Lord Jesus,' if you really mean it, He'll come in. That's how simple it is."

"Okay," she said, and I could hear her sniffing away tears.

"Jesus, forgive me for my sins," I prayed, saying the same simple words that every person on earth needs to say. "Come into my heart, Lord Jesus, and live through me. And when this life is over, take me home to be with You forever."

Maxine thanked me again and again for calling, and we hung up. I had scheduled a trip out of state for the next few days. When I returned, there was a message waiting for me at the campus switchboard. It was from the hospital.

"Maxine is gone, but she left a word for you. She said to say: 'Tell Aggie that all is well.' "

All is very well indeed.

Not An Epilogue

(*Written for Aggie by Doug Brendel*)

It was too beautiful a day for a funeral, and Erich said so. Less than a week before his seventh birthday, he was full of energy.

"I wish it had been a crummy day," he said, shifting restlessly in his brown plaid jacket. "I just want to get this over with and go home."

The people around him laughed. Aggie, too, would have complained about wasting such a terrific day at a funeral.

The group standing around Erich had just come from a hillside where they had lain Aggie Hurst to rest. Now they were waiting to go into the memorial service in the chapel at Northwest College, where hundreds of Aggie's friends were gathering. It was backwards this way—the burial first, then the memorial service. But Aggie would have enjoyed the ruination of this solemn tradition.

On the hillside, Pastor Charles Anderson had struggled

through all the proper funeral phrases, sounding appropriately solemn and hopeful. Finally, as the graveside service drew to a close, he blurted out a phrase that was really most accurate:

"She was a neat little lady."

Again and again, from the day of her death through the final reception memorializing her, the phrase would be repeated. She was such a neat lady. There had been none like her—and yet, in a sense, everyone was a bit like her.

That was how she related so easily to everyone she met. People recalled examples, such as the episode in the airport at Damascus, Syria. She was traveling to the Holy Land with a group from the college and, like the rest of the party, was tired from the long trip. The atmosphere in the airport was not especially friendly, and everyone stood around uneasily until customs could be cleared—except Aggie. She spotted a Jordanian mother, wrapped in traditional garments, sitting on the floor against a wall, holding one infant and tending another next to her. Aggie went directly to the woman, sat down next to her in exactly the same fashion, and began chattering happily. The mother smiled and answered—in Arabic. Neither woman spoke a word of the other's language, but neither minded. Soon they were talking like old friends, each in her own tongue, and Aggie was playing with the babies. She had found that common ground. She always did.

As Aggie began work on her book, she started having problems with her hip. At first she thought the old arthritis was flaring up, and prescribed herself a heating pad to sit on. It did not help. Soon her doctor had diagnosed the problem: the cancer had reappeared.

In rapid succession Aggie underwent more chemotherapy, another operation, and seven biopsies. The cancer was microscopic—as if it were timid about returning to plague such a "neat lady"—but it was there nonetheless. X-rays revealed new spots on her lungs and liver. Then came blood poisoning as a side effect of her condition. Phlebitis, an old nemesis, returned, and finally hermorrhaging led to a stroke, robbing her of speech and writing abilities.

She was flawlessly courageous through every new disaster. Her doctor expressed astonishment that she never slipped into depression. He had never seen another patient go through so much and retain such hope and peace.

So even in this extreme situation, Aggie had a way of helping others. She often quoted a simple platitude when friends were facing crises: "The birds will sing again." Now in her very attitude she quoted it for herself, for her family. She knew no despair. Hopeful mottos could be found all over her house, taped to the refrigerator, tacked to the bulletin board, fixed to the counter top. Many were borrowed from Dr. Robert Schuller, author and minister, whose positive outlook on life suited Aggie just fine: "It's always too soon to quit" ... "Turn your scars into stars" ... "Never say never" ... "God is greater than any problems I have." One day she jotted Schuller's credo in her Bible, a credo that sounded as if it were written just for her:

"When faced with a mountain I will not quit, I will keep on striving until I climb over, find a pass through, tunnel underneath, or simply turn the mountain into a gold mine, with God's help."

She had that tenacity. As the deterioration of her body progressed, the doctor knew better than to write Aggie off.

"She's a tiger," he told Dewey. "She'll fight to live as long as there's breath!"

The time came when the doctor had done all he could. He recommended that the family take her home and make her as comfortable as possible. For days son Rick and son-in-law Darrell maintained a vigil. They talked with Aggie, prayed with her, enveloped their mom in love.

No one clung to her soul. She was ready to meet Jesus, and the family was ready, too. Her earthly body refused to keep her—she deserved better: a heavenly body!

The whole family was there, listening as Pastor Anderson read Isaiah 40:31: "But they that wait upon the Lord shall renew their strength; they shall mount up with wings as eagles; they shall run, and not be weary; and they shall walk, and not faint."

Unable to speak, Aggie lifted her hands in praise to God. Then, she reached out to Gigi and Rick. The whole family joined hands around the bed, and Pastor Anderson read from 2 Corinthians 4:

"But we have this treasure in earthen vessels, that the excellency of the power may be of God and not of us. We are troubled on every side, yet not distressed; we are perplexed, but not in despair; persecuted, but not forsaken; cast down, but not destroyed; always bearing about in the body the dying of the Lord Jesus, that the life also of Jesus might be made manifest in our body.

"For we which live are always delivered unto death for Jesus' sake, that the life also of Jesus might be made manifest in our mortal flesh. So then death worketh in us, but life in you. . . .

"For our light affliction, which is but for a moment, worketh for us a far more exceeding and eternal weight of glory."

And then, the pastor read a few lines from Revelation 21:

"And I saw a new heaven and a new earth; for the first heaven and the first earth were passed away.... And God shall wipe away all tears from their eyes; and there shall be no more death, neither sorrow, nor crying, neither shall there be any more pain; for the former things are passed away."

Aggie went to sleep with her family encompassing her. She awoke in heaven.

The family determined to make the memorial service a time of praise to God, celebrating His gift of life—just as Aggie would have done if she could be there. Gigi laughed when she saw all the flowers covering the entire front of the chapel. Her mother would have said, "Get these flowers out of here! It looks like a funeral!"

"Maybe things would have been a little different if Aggie were here now," Pastor Anderson allowed as he opened the service.

"That's for sure!" Gigi whispered impishly to her dad. "We'd all be wearing dancing shoes and *dancing!*"

Dewey nodded and smiled, undoubtedly picturing Aggie wearing the finest of dancing shoes. How she had loved shoes, starting with the first pair she ever owned—the hand-me-downs that her brother David had outgrown in the Congo. Years later, in South Dakota, she had giggled excitedly whenever Dewey brought her sale shoes from the store. She was a size four-and-a-half, and any good shoe looked lovely in that tiny version.

Both Rick and Darrell sold shoes for several years as well, but it was Rick who made a living of it. It was a career much approved by Aggie.

When she came home from the hospital the last time she

was unable to walk. But in time, perhaps, the doctor believed that she might be able to take a few steps. The old problem of the weak right angle had surfaced again—the symptoms of rickets making their final appearance after all those years. The doctor ordered special shoes to be sent to the Hurst residence. They were plain, square-toed, brown. They were tiny—size fives, the smallest made by the company—but still bigger than Aggie had ever worn. And the right one was attached to a tall, metal brace, equipped with a leather strap, all of which would keep that crooked ankle straight.

Aggie never put them on.

Rick had told Dewey that one afternoon when he was alone with his mother she had asked him a painful question. The words were difficult to form and it took her a long time to get the question out.

"Rick, will I ever have pretty shoes again?"

Rick bit back his tears and smiled softly at her.

"You sure will," he replied.

Her son would never slip another shoe onto her tiny foot. But in Dewey's thoughts even the finest shoes in Rick's store could not compare to what Aggie would have now. When she breathed her last breath, she went exuberantly into heaven—and, if Aggie had her way, she probably *would* be wearing dancing shoes. Pretty ones.

Along with Pastor Anderson, Northwest District Superintendent Frank Cole and Tacoma Pastor Fulton Buntain officiated. Fulton could not keep a half-grin from forming throughout his entire tribute.

"Aggie discovered a secret of life that we seldom discover," he said. "And that secret was *having fun*. She was a free spirit." What delighted him most was Aggie's way of "poking holes in our religious pomposities, and pulling us religious types down off our perches."

Fulton sighed, and paid her the ultimate tribute.

"I would like my life to be more like hers."

The weather had been nonstop beautiful since the day Aggie left the hospital—a rare thing for Seattle in mid-March. The sunlight streamed through the chapel windows. But this lovely day, Fulton pointed out, was an absolutely miserable and contemptible day by Aggie's new heavenly standards.

She had indeed begun a new day. Her life was not a movie, but rather a serial. Instead of "The End," it was "To Be Continued." She had awakened from her slumber and found herself in heaven, completely healthy, happy, free to run again, to laugh and play, her true exuberant self.

Dewey's faith had been impacted as never before. He hated to see Aggie go, but he also hated to see her stay—so helpless. He loved to watch her swoop into a gathering and begin telling story after story. He loved to see her devotion to her children, and then her children-in-law, and then her grandchildren. He loved her even more as he observed in her a refinement process wrought through sickness. Each day, it seemed, was a new miracle of inner healing.

Dewey had stood by her bedside and strengthened her through five major surgeries in a space of eight years. There were extractions each time—actually *less body* after each operation—and yet he marveled to see how it all worked together to make her a *whole person*. It was in times of sickness or stress that Aggie pursued the power and presence of God.

Dewey told of the "real" Aggie coming to the surface and

illustrated the point with a story about Gigi and Rick. Rick was five years old, Gigi was less than ten, and Rick was the fly in his sister's ointment. He took great delight in infuriating her. One day Gigi stomped into the house after a particularly frustrating encounter with her brother.

"Mother!" she exclaimed. "How in the world could you *have* such a kid?"

Rick, meanwhile, had pursued other interests. He headed for the neighbor's swingset, which was not mounted securely, and promptly climbed to the top of the apparatus. He began swinging back and forth, courageously, until suddenly the whole thing tilted, throwing Rick to the ground and landing on top of him.

Gigi happened to see it through a window. She screamed for her mother. Then, without thinking, the real Gigi surfaced.

"Jesus!" she cried. "My only brother!"

The real Aggie had surfaced in much the same way. Her spiritual growth was most apparent in times of crisis. As Dewey observed her, worked alongside her, and supported her in prayer, Aggie became a true minister of Christ's grace. Although she never carried a minister's credentials, friends and strangers traveled hundreds of miles to see her, to be helped by her. She made a tape of her testimony, and almost incessantly she received letters from people who had experienced miracles in their lives after hearing Aggie tell her story. After decades of identity crises, the real Aggie had finally arrived.

Now, Dewey sat between his two children as the memorial service drew to a close. Anderson, Cole, and Buntain, three of his close colleagues in the ministry, had paid their public respects. Lola Bixler, who had sung at his inauguration as college president years before, stood to sing a final song.

God be with you till we meet again. . . .

Dewey put his arms around Gigi and Rick and bowed his head, squinting hard. His face grew red against his light hair, and the inside corners of his glasses steamed up just a bit. In the back of his throat, a lump seemed to choke him.

Then, holding his children, he said farewell to Aggie in his heart. And he cried.

In her Bible, Aggie left expressions of love for each member of her family. None were left out. She was in her entirety a person who loved.

On the nightstand by her bed she left a note, apparently written several weeks before her death. Its message clearly came from someone with a practical, unencumbered outlook on life—and yet above all, the hope of a wonderful future:

"What if I die? Well, it has not been in vain. I've had a good year—I'm looking forward to another good year.

"I don't want to die. I don't want to leave my husband and children, or my grandchildren.

"But on the other hand, if I die, I'll die in the arms of Jesus.

"And besides, look at all the wonderful people waiting for me. A mother I've *never* seen, my dear Aunt Signe, Grandma Hanson, Grandpa Hanson, Grandpa Hurst."

And then Aggie wrote a line, stark but true, with a hidden wisdom that comes from the fight for life:

"Everyone is terminal."

The family discussed Aggie's book at length. It was only a few minor revisions away from being finished when she died. How to end it? Joyfully, they decided.

But it was soft-spoken Rick who made the most forceful point.

"A lot of books have epilogues," he said. "No epilogue for Mom's book. This is no ending. This is a new beginning."

Young Erich had been entertaining himself in the midst of the family gathering following the memorial service when suddenly he looked up and spoke for everyone.

"I wish Jesus had taken *this* cancer away," he said. "Grandma got cancer before, but Jesus took it away. This time He didn't, and she went to heaven. I wish she was here now."

But then, as if to underscore Rick's point of new beginnings, Erich glanced around with a glint of his grandmother's smile, looked at the table filled with food, and said, "Come on, let's eat. I'm hungry. Wanna see my new yo-yo trick?" he asked. "Watch this!"

Not The End